Joy Beyond The Walls Of This World:

Healing The Souls Of Men . . . And Women

Dr. James E. McReynolds
Minister Of Joy To The World

Joy Beyond The Walls Of This World: Healing The Souls Of Men . . . And Women
ISBN: Softcover 978-1-955581-43-1
Copyright © 2021 by James E. McReynolds

All rights reserved. No part of this book may be reproduced or transmitted in any form or by any means, electronic or mechanical, including photocopying, recording, or by any information storage and retrieval system, without permission in writing from the publisher.

Parson's Porch Books is an imprint of Parson's Porch & Company (PP&C) in Cleveland, Tennessee. PP&C is an innovative organization which raises money by publishing books of noted authors, representing all genres. Its face and voice is **David Russell Tullock** (dtullock@parsonsporch.com).

Parson's Porch & Company *turns books into bread & milk* by sharing its profits with the poor.

www.parsonsporch.com

Other Books by James McReynolds Published by Parson's Porch Books

The Spirituality of Joy: The Least Discussed Human Emotion

The Joy of Preaching: Encountering Jesus through the Word of God

Dancing with God: A Theology of Joy

The Silence of the Church: The Spiritual Struggle with Sexuality

The Spirit of Joy Church

Joy Comes in the Mourning: Love Is Forever

The Joy of Prayer: The Way to Intimacy with God

The Joy of the Kingdom: Envisioning the Great Commission

Joy in the Seasons of Life: Walking Each Other Home to God

Living the Dream: Amazing Adventure in Marriage

Joy Beyond the Walls of This World: Healing the Souls of Men . . .and Women

Foreword By Dr. John Killinger

James McReynolds has been my friend for more than 50 years. I am always amazed at the vastness of his knowledge, and his curiosity about most everything.

He manages to bring it all into the years of service and global ministry of the one great and constant theme of his heart, which is the joy of life itself.

His flame runs steadily, and it burns with truth and love. I sincerely believe that this book is the finest he has written. No reader could come away from it without feeling all his senses joyfully atingle with excitement. People who read this book chapter by chapter will want to apply this or that insight garnered from reading it.

Thank you, Jim, for your unswerving devotion to this important subject, and for the inspiration you have provided to us to see the wonderful joy in our midst, and to do everything we can to release it as a blessing upon the world.

This book is the sleeper of a decade.

John Killinger
Warrenton, Virginia

DEDICATION

To all the beautiful and talented women in my life who have brought me joy and who have added their talents to bring happiness, peace, music, fun, and laughter during my life journey in all its glorious seasons.

My loving wife Laurel, my daughter Linda, my bonus daughters Carmen and Carrie, my awesome bonus granddaughters Brooke, Jillian, Cameryn, McKenzie, great granddaughters Sky, Nova, and Aurora, who have blessed my life immensely.

Contents

Foreword By Dr. John Killinger 5
Dedication 7
Introduction 11
Chapter One 27
   Balancing Masculine and Feminine Energy 27
Chapter Two 45
   Understanding Joy 45
Chapter Three 62
   Surrendering for Joy 62
Chapter Four 71
   Cultivating Joy in Relationships 71
Chapter Five 86
   Enhancing Joy for the Masculine Soul 86
Chapter Six 94
   Loving the Gift of a Man's Daughter or Son 94
Chapter Seven 105
   Walking Each Other Home 105
Chapter Eight 113
   The Author's Personal Transformation 113
Chapter Nine 125
   Living in Joy in the Here and Now 125
Chapter Ten 134
   Life Is Not A Competition 134
Afterword 143
Bibliography 145
About the Author 152

INTRODUCTION

Society is changing rapidly. This is a book about men. It is also about women. It's about crises in human life. Economic and social pressures have never been as vast. We all live in confusion, in ego-based defenses. We all need to be loved. Love knows no sexual, racial, political, religious, or anything else. Women and men are having a difficult time understanding each other.

The gender crisis can become an opportunity for men and women to discover their true selves. We need to reach our human potential. Every child of God has been imbued and reflects how that potential has waxed and waned throughout history.

The soul exists irrespective of its human form. Each gender has an inner essence. It is the will of God that we allow masculine and feminine free expression. Our current gender crisis curtails our potential as joyful partners. We have lost sight of this truth. Our joint vision quest moves beyond constrictive gender forms.

This crisis has gone on too long and we must create new visions.

John Killinger wrote two novels about a woman named Jessie. Jessie is an artist. She paints parables instead of telling them. Jessie gets into trouble with the conservative and fundamental religious establishments by doing a series of portraits of women in religion. Her work gets her crucified. She is dismissed by church authorities just as feisty women are in our day. They cannot silence her. She is a Christ-like woman, especially when she turns water into the best beer anyone ever tasted. John's novel is a believable parable of how God transcends gender.

Killinger wrote a second novel titled *The Night Jessie Sang at the Opry*. The women in my family and my female clergy colleagues loved it.

Jessie writes and sings songs about life and people and the evil in today's culture. Better than a host of sermons, the book is an allegory of the life of Jesus told in contemporary terms. In *The Night Jessie Sang at the Opry*, the sequel to is first novel, Jessie returns to life as a country music singer in Nashville, Tennessee. Nashville is called "the Vatican City of America," because of its numerous religious headquarters. She issues a compelling call to righteousness and honesty on the religious scene. Immediately she is confronted with staunch resistance from quite a number of highly placed church leaders. Nashville is the nearest thing to Jerusalem, perfect for a message about a female Christ.

The Academy Award winning movie *Chocolat* is a summary of what I'm sharing in this book. The novel and the movie are crammed full of visual metaphors. I insist you see the movie or get a DVD and read or see it from beginning to end. Each character illuminates the reality of the transformations needed in today's world. Alphonse Marceau represents all weary husbands.

Serge Muscat is the drunken café owner. There is a retired man, a woman suffering from diabetes, a tradition bound priest, a wife starving for physical affection, and a widow.

We see the healing of a masculine soul in Comte de Reynaud, the dominating mayor of Lasquenet. Joanne Harris published the novel *Chocolat* in 2000. The book is set in our present day. The movie setting is in the 1950s.

The leading role is a journeying chocolate maker. Anouk is her daughter.

Few find the joy of living. The results we create come about from how we live. The process of acceptance is difficult. The issues are staggering, complex, critical. Writing this book was not an easy task. I am not prepared to discuss what I have been compelled to live through, to access the wounds, to gain some level of understanding. My few insights are only a drop in the ocean to what must be known.

The imaginary French town is like most communities, especially religious ones. Those who control and those who are controlled have an unspoken pact. Vianne, the feisty stranger, refuses to accept the norms of the town. She throws much confusion and challenges. Like Jesus, she challenged the statis quo, and refused to follow church traditions. The church, then and now, is perceived as the most authoritarian and hierarchal when it comes to transformation of the world.

The goal of ministers should be to bring an atmosphere of joy to the world. Those bishops, presbytery executives, regional ministers, associational missionaries, or whatever must become more flexible and accountable. They should become open to question and open to change.

Both male and female pastors say the only way is to dismantle the old structures and create new ones. This is happening in places society is not aware of. The Reformation aimed to transform. After leaving the Catholic church, new groups split and split into innumerable denominations, movements, and ego centered groups with their own set of rules. Read Matthew 23.

Chocolat gives a voice to the common view of religion in our time. Religion is mistrusted because it leads to oppression not freedom. Vianne is a Christ figure. She refuses to be intimidated and she shows her defiance. Vianne is a picture of joy, and the town and church doors are opened. Comte de Reynaud quickly shuts her down. He only thinks of keeping his world safe and contained, keeping life as he thinks the whole world needs to be. Read Revelation 3:19-20.

This book, perhaps like *Chocolat*, will not be an easy read. My own opinions and beliefs are not important. This writing is to stimulate, to stir the apathetic, to heal the masculine soul. Women are rediscovering their power. And so are black folks who are quickly outnumbering white skinned people.

A new world is forming. The changes include our family and friends, all races and genders. Our interactions will be with all humankind. Of course, the male ego has taken a beating. It is a waste of time and energy to look toward repairing the ego to historical patterns. We must create new understandings of the way in which the ego works for and against us. Those past glories were not as great as some think. We must all understand how we fit into and beyond this world we created.

When I served as a writer and communication specialist in 1970 at the Sunday School Board of the Southern Baptist Convention, the executive president, James L. Sullivan, asked me to read *Future Shock*. One thing I thought about was in Alvin Toffler's words: "Change is here on our heads and most people are grotesque and unprepared to cope with it." (Alvin Toffler, *Future Shock*, p. 12)

It is important that males become aware that women appear determined to find their answers with us or without us. Based on current world conditions, we really have no choice but to transform ourselves immediately. The walls of this world will fall. As a species, humans are doomed if we take no action now.

Albert Einstein said it well, "No problem can be solved from the same level of consciousness that created it."

Men fear releasing the tenderness buried in their souls. Men fear the feminine in themselves. Men sense the ambivalence between wanting to hold on to aggression and wanting retaliation when it is not necessary nor appropriate.

During the 1980's, I conducted Healing the Masculine Soul support groups. Some revealed that they had learned to trust enough "to be fertilized by another man's soul." A strong healing black man summarized his transformation, "I am not worried about what life did not bring to me."

Power over your mind, not outside culture is where we find strength. Focus on what you can do now, not what you have not been permitted to do. Transformation gets us into a different attitude. This joy is painted into each day with practice.

Interdependence is must more effective than independence. We value "me" over the "we." For years psychology has insisted that self-love is the key to flourishing. Loving oneself requires one also be able to love other people. Men and women who become psychologists and psychiatrists to learn to cope with life themselves. In my practice, I have come to realize that marriage and family therapy works better than individual therapy. Most therapists deal with the dark side. They try to root out what is wrong with a person. The goal of psychotherapy (healing of the soul) is not to delve into misery, but to find joy.

Nobody experiences too much joy.

Nobody can experience too much joy. Containing joy leads us to lose sight of the human joy response. Living in joy brings peace, not matter how we are behaving. Joy is contagious. It heals us and others as well. Being joyful is not a means for denying suffering in our changing world. We cannot solve any relationship problems in this world community until we are able to become joyful. Our nation and every nation on earth would be transformed beyond the plastic smiles and shallow promises of prosperity and power to a real concern for joy to rule the world. We are less likely to elect another Adolph Hitler who leads us into a senseless war, injustice laws, and more misery for all except those given too much power.

Help your spouse today. Visit a nursing home, hospice, or prison. Your body and soul calmness when you help somebody else. Using your energy for other people will bring you joy. It is up to you my beloved readers to alter the way we walk together through life.

Take the way many people await an Armageddon that must happen before there is salvation. The world tends to become as we choose to see it. We are eternal pessimists. We set the stage for whatever happens to us. Negative rumors travel faster than positive rumors. Lies are believed more than facts if that is what we desire. Pity parties are easier for religionists and prohibitionists than reaching for joy.

Men are coping with rapid change in our culture. Men can rise above their negative past experiences. We were created to experience joy beyond the walls of this world. We cannot create, nor would we want to relive the past. We can only start this moment to create a better future. Let us begin with the physical reality of life. Adam gave his woman the name Eve, which means "the life-giving one." Read Genesis 3:20.

Life Begins at Conception

When I can share my concepts of joy, I discuss life at the Basilica of Conception near Maryville, Missouri. They appear to keep repeating, "Life begins at Conception."

The first nine months of our lives took place in our mother's womb. The early shaping of our existence was in the womb. We were a part of our mother's body.

Whatever your mother ate, you ate. When she held a feeling, you held it too. Her life limited yours. If she lived, you lived. If she died, you died.

Few have any memory as an embryonic child of their fathers. Science reveals that a newborn infant might in a sense "recognize" its father. They heard the voice while *in utero* from outside the womb. There is a spiritual bond that comes with conception. The relationship with the father from outside our human life is remote, tenuous, and intangible.

Resent research indicates that the unborn child is profoundly affected by and responds emotionally and physically from stimuli including sounds of life such as music or even reading to the child. When my daughter Linda was in her mother's womb, my wife was a student at Belmont University in Nashville. During a lively concert, her mother could feel her kicking inside.

The Bible confirms this as John the Baptist stirred within his mother Elizabeth's womb when Mary, pregnant with Jesus, stood with Elizabeth. Read Luke 1:41-44.

John somehow recognized Jesus even when both were living in the womb. Human life recognizes and responds to spiritual reality, including child and father.

This has profound implications for the male child's later relationships with women. The first woman a man loves is his mother. Recognizing and accepting this truth of a man's utter dependence on a woman may project the dependence and the accompanying fear onto the woman he loves as an adult. Nothing is more repulsive to a woman than a desperate man.

Life does not depend on a woman. It does not depend on a woman's male lover. "The joy of the Lord is your strength" as we are re-born into the kingdom of God.

Read John 3:5-6. Peter also says the same. Read I Peter 1:23. Women coming out of their own infancy assume the role of primary vitality when they become wives and mothers. When the family is falling apart within, nine times out of ten, the woman responds by calling clergy or counselors for help. Living with her vast feminine energy, women can become exhausted. Women experience healing and freedom as they surrender their attempts to fulfill the traditional roles for women. Elementary school has a feminine environment dominated by female authority figures. Sunday School is the same. The church activities are not what boys enjoy.

The church offers little help. Church has become secularized. Church is now feminized with less and less involvement of men. Church is not capable of being a part of healing the masculine soul.

There needs to be an appropriate starting point in our quest for a model for masculine affirmation. Women have many entry points to becoming a part of the body of Christ. I have found it difficult but needed to organize a men's group in church. My wife is active in church through the United Methodist Women, the food bank, monthly dinners, community projects, church boards, the church's lay leader, music director, book club member, UMW church conference projects, so many to occupy her time and enjoying feminine engagements that do not involve men. My wife Laurel enjoys books as much as I do. She has more books on womanist theology than any woman I know. We often read in each other's collections. She has a female book club through her church. Her bell choir and the sanctuary choir is made up mostly of females. Her pastor is a female.

As pastor for Saint Luke United Methodist Church in Bristol, Virginia, the men experienced little joy. I organized a golf outing on Saturdays where we played "best ball." It was a fun and spiritually rich experience. "Best ball" in golf means that no matter how limited a men's talent for golf, only the best ball, the ball near he target counted. We played in groups of four with the most athletic men were placed into each group. Do any of you readers remember those old pictures of as many as 200 men in the men's Sunday School class on the walls or histories of the church?

Embracing Change in a Time of Uncertainty

Men and women are now grappling with the fact that any new normal is not what it was. Nobody can consciously control outside sources such as wars, the economy, and pandemics. The only thing we can control is how we respond, interpret, and react.

We must accept rapid changes and embrace change without fear. We are in a time of rapid changes that makes it nearly impossible to navigate. There is stigma about asking for help and cooperation. We celebrate personal independence. We have tortured ourselves as we search for answers. We must unlock our power to support
the quest for fulfilling your destiny. My wife has served as a registered nurse for more than 50 years. When we moved to Nebraska, she wanted to put her skills to use. A job opening

appeared in the Lincoln Star newspaper for a position as the director of nursing for the Dialysis Centers of Lincoln, Nebraska.

As she contemplated the possibility, she did not apply. She had so many gifts and she did talk with her friends and mentors including her most recent position in mental health nursing at Woodridge Psychiatric Center in Johnson City, Tennessee. With prayer, renewed confidence, and her husband's support, she decided to apply. She sure needed my support, so I helped her create a resume and turned it in to the center in Lincoln. She was given an interview and she impressed the administration, and they offered the job.

Laurel stepped into the biggest vision of her career. Her ability to relate and manage nurses was exponential. She found herself in a fast lane. Everything began to accelerate. She succeeded even with the multi-taking and demanding head administrator, her boss. She continued to be accountable by showing up in ways that were consistent with her commitment. She found support inside herself to realize her potential. Her strength and trust in God activated a deeper possibility for who she was created to be.

The fierce urgency of now.

Oppression of both men and women must not remain uncontested. We must act.

Martin Luther King wrote of the "fierce urgency of now." The present world is intense, fascinating, and challenging. We are deeply divided racially, sexually, and politically. It is deeply troubling. There are many sides to every issue. Look at how we divide politically. Conservatives want to save the past and future as do liberals. Many men and women support each ideological viewpoint. We see this played out in the news media. Some just turn it off or watch only one side's networks. This impacts how we relate to each other. We can even understand which side our multi-thousand denominations are on. This book and my words are not about politics.

The way we engage each other is vital. How we debate and discuss our being right reveals the divide. We must find common ground if anything is accomplished. Our current political and cultural climate, as well as the rise of important social movements has focused awareness to those problems involving race, inequality, privilege, and gender. We can no longer opt out of addressing these issues. Those issues are difficult, uncomfortable, and confusing.

Unless we include everyone can hold feelings that all are cherished. God gave each person a place. Each one owns themselves as children of God. We have a common bond, so we need not compete for involvement or being included with inherent dignity and grace. Many men try to do ministry or other work by themselves. The crisis has proven living in joy in this world is an equal opportunity phenomenon.

The population of the earth grows dramatically each day. We lament the plague of relationship problems. From our very beginning, friendships have been destroyed, marriages have become broken, churches have been dissolved, and multitudes of wars have been fought because of our breaks in relationships.

The role of gender cannot be overlocked. Freedom of self-expression is limited. The way we are being taught about gender issues play a major role in social ills, such as purging teenage girls, suicides of adolescent boys, number of men in our prisons, and mass shootings. Only one perpetrators of mass killings were a woman.

Our greatest danger is from ourselves. Apart from the intervention of God, humans now threaten to extinguish every one of us from the earth. We have never found how-to live-in harmony. Divided people cannot recognize their imperfections. We have endangered our own existence. Read Proverbs 6:16-19. The problems will not fade away.

Collegiality is being prudent. This human virtue insists that everyone participates in the shared mission. We need to refrain spending time bemoaning problems. Do question majority decisions and blind voting. During the years I served as the moderator for the regional board of the Christian Church (Disciples of Christ) in Nebraska, I experienced the board members become easily taken in with no questioning votes hat hurt everyone in the end.

Fifty years ago, there were virtually no women leading congregations as pastors in the United States except in a few Pentecostals and a handful of mainline churches. Many seminaries had not yet admitted women to the basic bachelor of divinity degree.

By 2021 women are serving as pastor in nearly ever denomination with notable exceptions of the two largest: Roman Catholics and Southern Baptists. Untold numbers of women have left these groups to become leaders in other denominations.

For the past three decades, women's power has risen dramatically. Women's seminary enrollments have peaked, especially among black women. Mainline denominations now have a burgeoning growth in pastors who identify themselves as lesbian, gay, bisexual, trans, intersex, or queer.

The simultaneous growth in women's leadership and the widespread decline of Protestant churches, where most female pastors serve need further exploration. The places where women remain excluded or marginalized as pastors and priests provide a stark contrast to the vibrant ministries of women.

As more women attend seminaries and continue to serve prevalence status among those who oversee the gates for calling or appointing pastors, many biblical interpretations surrounding it will continue. Seminaries have changed in curriculum, requirements, and clot. Quite a few have been closed for lack of support. Baptist Theological Seminary in Richmond, Virginia is one example. Many seminaries now award a degree for students who do their work online.

Amy Butler was selected as pastor of the Riverside Church in New York, Shannon Kershner the first senior pastor for Fourth Presbyterian Church in Chicago, and Ginger Gaines for the Foundry United Methodist Church in Washington. There is not a city in America where women are not now pastors.

Many theological seminaries would not exist without their female students. The bachelor of divinity degree was replaced by the master of divinity. The degree no longer requires competence in Greek and Hebrew, biblical studies, church history, and other subjects. Seminaries reduced requirements and added the doctor of ministry to give graduates more prestige and equaling with physicians and lawyers. The administrations of seminaries worked frantically with these issues in order to survive.

As increasing numbers of women enter the ordained ministry embrace and challenge traditional female roles. Clergywomen are changing aspects of the ministry. *The Review of Religious Research* is published four times each year. It provides a regular channel for the exchange of information on methods, findings, a variety of articles, book reviews, and trends in church leadership.

With family and friends, share the vision for who you can become. Think about pondering your life right now. Imagine a year from now, having unlocked any limits and awakened your feminine and masculine soul. What is possible? Visualize what your true best self looks like. Read Proverbs 11:25.

The door to joy is unlocked by using the keys of God. Joy in ministry is an inside joy. God calls humans into ministry that is obtainable, abundant, tangible, and possible.

Collegiality has benefits. It develops decision makers. It protects the church and other organizations from egregious misrule or a dictatorship. Hitler was voted in as chancellor of Germany. He became the master of everything. He overestimated his own capacities and underestimated all others. He was overly sensitive, mistrustful. He eliminated and blamed any person or group that opposed him.

The continuity of a nation or of the world is assured only if leaders promote their organization or church rather than themselves. Dictators come and go. So do we. No human is indispensable.

I know I have not felt any need to use my own desires to obtain any ministries. Often, I have received a surprising phone call or letter asking me to consider serving a church or institution needing my skills and graces.

There are not many prayer meetings in today's congregations. Communication through prayer brings release from trying to handle life alone. Prayer builds trust in God, not in systems, and opens our lives to the grace of God. Grace cleanses our lives. The love of God calls us to the Lord wiping away the dust. With both male and female spirituality, e ae free from the difficulties, bondages, and failures. By surrendering our fragile egos, your life is filled with joy.

Despite your gender or your assumed power, we must fill ourselves with courage, energies, love-filled change, support, encouragement, affirmation, and contentment. We are freed to love all others with the assurance that God loves us. We see Christ in each human being. We serve humanity for the sake of God.

Peace flows through submission, not resignation. Called pastors are victors not victims. Men and women have been hit by life's storms. We must communicate with God to overcome gender troubles or build new walls. Christ talked to God about his life's path before he moved to acceptance. We can choose our response to life's changes with the help of God. Joy is our choice to think of life as a blessing.

Simply choosing positive thoughts is not enough for joy.

We are required to be proactive rather than reactive to impact the world. We choose the thoughts that direct our actions. If we are reactive, needs and wants, power-seeking, will destroy our character. Our inflated egos are the cause for us to do something that is wrong but feels right from our perspective. Entering the world of wrong thinking causes the current reactions. Life eventually will fall apart. Negative thinking can be redirected at any time, before, during, of after negative, immoral, or wrong actions. Proactive brings the joy to impact the world. Reactive is the way we react to life as it slams into us.

Focus on the possibilities or we will be consumed by impossibilities. Read Mark 9:2-11. Christ's disciples responded to unexpected change in the same ways we tend to do today. Those men were stunned by the unearthly appearance of Jesus. This was an exciting, unexpected moment. Positive unexpected change causes the same reaction as negative unexpected change. Joy depends on where we focus. Prayer centers us. The most helpful way to find clear sight is to balance our feminine and masculine energy.

Keep in mind that we are personally responsible for becoming more ethical than the culture we grew up in. There is a difference in "serving in order to gain" and "gaining in order to serve."

Self-serving leaders are dominated by the wrong motives. They will serve s long as they can gain. Then they just stop. They are no longer available. A culture of service increases our passion to adapt to radical change in the environment. Our life journeys will include fabulous joy and heart-wrenching pain. Life is not an easy path. We underestimate ourselves, but God never does. God knows what exactly what we are capable of, and the world needs us now.

In our frenetically evolving marketplace and volatile world, we could be forgiven for feeling pushed back into a wait-for-normal-to-come-back corners. We are peering anxiously to see when the wise moment to transform ourselves into our joy-filled lives.

The world is a wall of loss, chaos, media power, community division. This book aims to help you set the stage to transcend the status-quo and claim your highest life.

Chapter One

Balancing Masculine and Feminine Energy

Humans bristle when certain qualities such as assertive, dominant, rigid, powerful, closed, negative, serious, anxiety, control, judgement, left brain, selfishness, yang, and verbal are designated as male. Energy forms for female include flowing, subtle, soft, open. Supportive. Positive. Playful. Surrender. Excellence. Spontaneity. Acceptance. Joy. Right brain. Yin. Visual.

The Chinese say the journey of a thousand miles begins not just with the first step, but with putting your traveling shoes on. Time moves on whether we are productive in energetic balance. Rituals. Routines. Habits. Mastery. Push energy right now.

Power is confusing. Human beings embrace it and recoil from it at the same time. Females say they are tired of being used. The become angry and demanding. Men might just be wimpy or passive. Relationships continue to be misunderstood. Balancing power is a problem. Struggles for power are framed in personal transformation. This struggle begins the day we are born. Healthy balanced power feels like wholeness. It respects self and others. Say no, say yes, accept and go on with life. Mother Teresa said, "Not all of us can do great things. But we can still small things with great love."

"Our job as women is to relearn glory for living attuned to the feminine radar," Marianne Williamson said. The key to meeting the need to visualize your daughters as adults. Every person's soul is the same we had at age 2, 20, 80, or on our last day of our lives. (Marianne Williamson, *A Woman's Worth*, pp. 110-113)

The women's movement reacts negatively to chauvinism, a compensating overreaction. Aggression results when on an inner level of some men who feel women have greater power than he. Environmental and traditional experiences Mothers and women companions are often dominant figures in a male's life.

This energy imbalance serves women no better than men. Women want the energies to be balanced. Men resist aggressive women, and they refuse to change.

Energy patterns shift. Women have sensed when the negative, hardline masculine energy usurps the open softness of feminine energy.

The belief in the political, religious, and cultural equality of women existed in the earliest forms of civilization. The history is fascinating. Men must realize that the fight for women's suffrage to women's marches through the "Me Too" movement.

Greek, Roman, Egyptian, and oriental men reacted to the protests of women saying that as soon as women become your equals, they will soon become your superiors.

Abigail Adams, first lady to President John Adams, energized women's access to education, property, and the vote as critical to feminine equality. During the abolitionist movement discovered an unsettling irony in advocating for African Americans rights that they themselves were not allowed themselves.

A few women served as soldiers in the American Civil War. Susan B. Anthony and Carrie Catt worked tirelessly for the 19th amendment passed giving women the right to vote.

Just after that was completed, women began more waves of feminist work.

Women began to enter the workplace and leadership in churches and other institutions following the Great Depression. Single women were nurses, schoolteachers. During the Depression millions of male breadwinners lost their jobs. Women searched for low paying jobs such as housework or secretarial roles.

During World War II, women found work in industries previously done by men. The feminist icon in those days was called Rosie the Riveter. Some women served as nurses during the wars. When the war ended, men were sent to Korea to serve military operations. The civil rights movement stirred women to greater participation in workplaces with equal pay as a major goal for their efforts.

Cultural obstacles remained. Betty Friedan wrote *The Feminine Mystique* in 1963. The Equal Pay Act passed that same year. Gloria Steinem organized the National Women's Political Caucus in 1971.

Women argued that all the women's movements did was to limit all but white, college-educated women were the only ones who benefited.

By the 2010s, feminists pointed to the prominent cases of sexual assault and rape culture. In October 2017, the *New York Times* exposed sexual harassment against rich film maker Harvey Weinstein. Thousands of women came forward with their allegations against powerful men, including President Donald Trump.

On January 21, 2017, the first day of Trump's presidency, thousands of women joined a Women's March in Washington. There were more women and quite a few men were said to have outnumbered Trump's inauguration attenders. There were more than 10 million others worldwide who held demonstrations, providing feminists with high-profile platforms for advocating for rights for women.

The new understanding of feminine energy is going beyond the walls of our world with opportunities for making changes. The feminine in both men and women deeply wants to love and care. There is fertile ground for joy when we all accept that everyone has lessons to learn, while allowing others to learn their own. Read Mathew 14:13-21. "Not counting women and children." Has that not been true in cultures that women and children have not been counted? They are left out. What if some masculine dominating soul only counted men in lists of church membership, lists of ordained ministers, or the total who are feed spiritual food in church settings? The correct total of those who are in the feeding of the five thousand should be 35,000 hungry people.

Feminine energy refers to a specific set of traits. Our masculine side is expressing when we are making goals, making progress, getting things finished. Our feminine side is addressed when we exist with the flow of life, embrace your creative energy, play, dance, and attune to your inner self. Amelia Earhart noted, "Women must try to do things as men have tried. When they fail, their failure must be but a challenge to others."

Mary Piper is a psychotherapist who has given me my best thoughts. She teaches Psychology of Women and Sex Roles and Gender at the University of Nebraska in Lincoln. Her recent book has 253 pages we should not miss. She addresses women through all the ages of her life. She notes that in old age we will suffer losses. We will say goodbye to most everyone we love. She does vision quests for women including an annual All-Women's Camping Trip. Her group rides a boat down the Platte River which she says in a mile wide and an inch deep. Ice jams clog things up during Nebraska winters. She talks of the shoals and the logjams. In spring and summer as the rains come, it becomes a muddy swimming hole. She enjoys lush sunsets and the call of the wild geese as they float down the Platte River (Mary Piper, *Women Rowing North*, 174-178, 245-253)

These traits are not associated with gender.

Feminine stems from expectations that in the past we have defined in the past. Masculine stems from traits assigned for men in the same past. In the present time we know people of any gender have a combination of those traits. No certain traits are assigned to any gender. When writing about transformation to our true and best selves, the words "feminine" and "masculine" are needed in describing two different and opposing ways of being. Both energies are necessary for being a complete person. Joy and satisfaction come for every person to have outlets for both masculine and feminine energies. Until now, most people have been out of touch with feminine energy. This has the feeling of being off-balanced. Being overly masculine and under feminine leaves us longing for something else. We are missing something resourceful, something wild, something rejuvenating, something spontaneous. That's the feminine side. "In societies where men are truly confident of their worth, women are not merely tolerated but valued," wisely noted Aung San Suu Kyi.

Conversion comes from a life-altering experience. Courage sacrifices self for realizing just goals. Courage is not enough to act according to our conscience. Hitler and every terrorist acted on conscience. Courage means endurance. Even in times of upheaval, the integrity of conscience brings surprising joy.

My daughter used to say that she wanted to be "lady-like." That was her creative force. Lady-like women expressed this by dancing, writing, painting, playing music. Anything that expresses our flow is feminine energy. Women appear to have more emotional intelligence. Women in ministry have refused to become discouraged when the culture rejected them. Feminine energy that realizes masculine energy brings about constancy, not through words or dazzling propaganda. Courageous women know when to be discreet and when to see the power of being "lady-like." Angelina Jolie said, "Barefoot or first thing in the morning, I feel beautiful. I did not always feel that way, but I feel that way now. When somebody loves you, and when you make somebody else happy, you suddenly feel like the most beautiful person in the world."

Every human is born with yin and yang energies. We can lean toward one polarity or the other. After thousands of healing lessons, we know that nobody will attain a perfect balance of both energies. Each person is unique and special. We feel our experiences before understanding them. Feminine energy makes us honest, vulnerable, transparent, and our authentic real self. When energies are in balance, most people feel special in your presence. These are the ones who know and feel that they are totally understood by you. All the ideals in the world will amount to nothing without dominion over the ability to change and the agility to navigate changes around you. If we are not growing and changing, we are dying.

Processing Emotions

Expectations for emotional processing differ with males and females. More women are labeled "sensitive" than are men. It is acceptable for women to express feelings. Men are, for the most part, not encouraged to outwardly express emotions. Gender stereotypes have been part of culture for many generations. Men who express emotions are viewed as weak. Men are afraid of the possible repercussions. The suppression of emotions is seen as detrimental to men's health. Men tend to hide emotions. From early age, men are conditioned to believe that men do not show feelings. Men do have emotions. Research shows that men experience emotions at the same level that women do.

Men channel emotions feelings into different feelings such as anger. Grieving men are more likely to act aggressive over small things. Men's feelings are associated with power, strength, and dominance.

There are consequences for emotional avoidance. Mental health disorders such as anger mismanagement, generalized anxiety disorder, or clinical depression are the results. Men become quite effective in turning off emotion. The current cycle of toxic masculinity is almost impossible to break. Becoming vulnerable is hard if people have hidden feelings all their life. Vulnerability requires being honest about feelings. Men are less likely to see a therapist than women. Men commit suicide 400 times more than women do.

The continuing demand for the rights of women for equality is a battle for equal power. These successful strivings mean a loss of power for men. Men must recognize the destruction and confront this human poison. This means more than intensions. Life today is just too horrible when men cannot trust women and women cannot trust men. It is no way for us to live. It offends against justice. It will never work. All of us are responsible for all of us, all the time.

People cling to their ideologies. Both right and left must be enlisted in service of the vulnerable using language they will accept. Where is the equilibrium we need and accept? The world's walls are high and deep. Spoiling our day and experiencing the rocking of our world. Propensity for self-preoccupation, body chemistry, and internal reactions play havoc on our attempts to heal our souls.

Relax. Exhale. Breathe, and inhale equilibrium to find strength to build the kingdom of God on earth.

The human system is not capable of holding a full lifetime of suppressed emotions. Women express emotions more often and more readily. This feminine attribute is the single most important difference in the way men and women live. Jacqueline Bisset wrote, "Character contributes to beauty It fortifies a woman as her youth fades. A mode of conduct, a standard of courage, discipline, fortitude and integrity can do a great deal to make a woman beautiful."

I enjoy having my Laurel to help me in any workshops, teachings, and quests for igniting fires of joy. Women who Laurel has directed and supported at the Dialysis Centers rave about the impact unlocking their feminine power. She has been the key catalyst for transforming their self-esteem and their health. They begin to feel beautiful inside and out.

Laurel's own feminine power has liberated numerous women from self-doubt and insecurity. She and they attract true equals including myself to what all God's children most desire. We must tear down the world's walls blocking evolved women and men from realizing how great they are.

The subtle shift from this realization happens without our realizing what has happened. So, we retaliate toward the selfishness. Meeting other people's needs in cooperation the only way any of us will get our needs met.

We react out of our perceived needs, even if we are dead wrong. Like children, we are emotionally invested in the current issues that trouble us. We misunderstand each other. We shift from trusting that needs can be met to insisting they are met.

The fire of divine energy burns down walls.

Fire is a life-taking and life giving holding the power and passion of divine energy. Fire blazes through the walls of collective consciousness. Fire inspires the momentum already started. Fire is a symbol for warming our souls, for inciting us to move our bodies, lift the spirit, and to quicken our minds. The fire rooted in divine energy means to become untamed.

God is always reaching to us. The walls of the world are breaking down Walls block God out. God never leaves us, but we can leave God. The difference between trying to solve problems on our own and doing our journey with God is our gift of joy. Spiritual disease and wall building have kept us in negative joyless places.

The divide won't go away by itself. Women and men become creative in their quest for recognition. If we feel ignored, we attempt to play the guilty card. We keep score on the times we have been mistreated. With our imputing guilt approach, we discover it has changed nothing. Open and aggressive action is the next step. Humans will express emotions more and more. These emotional tactics are not a working panacea.

Wall-building is quiet, easy to justify, difficult to recognize the symptoms of walling God out. We become afraid, raged, depressed worried, bitter, sarcastic, rude, and insecure. We feel alone. Self-centeredness rather than other focusing controls us. Joylessness is perceived as someone else's fault. Tina Turner never blamed others for her limitations. "I didn't have anybody, really, no foundation in life, so I had to make it my own way. Always, from the start. I had to go out into the world and become strong, to discover my mission in life."

For every principle of cooperation, there is the opposite side of domination. To get our needs met through control methods, we think like a dominator. We no longer see each other as a person. Susan Sontag shared her view: "What is most beautiful in virile men is something feminine; what is most beautiful in feminine women is something masculine."

In retaliation, somebody gives up. That does not solve the problem. This kind of action moves the masculine-feminine issues deeper into degeneration. Flexibility is a requirement for us to walk in faith. Proper balance comes with God as our direction. Balancing the feminine and the masculine is tenuous. It is so difficult to find. It is difficult to keep.

Finding our purpose, our reason for being, is crucial to joy. We yearn for an identity. Joy happens and then it is another positive memory. We can be overwhelmed with our desperate searches for identity and purpose. Life experiences free us for our unique mission. God's perception of difficulties, challenges, and disappointments differs from our own view. Things we consider s curses can become blessings. Read Matthew25:14-26.

Jesus' parable of the talents infers that every person on earth has gifts, and each has the responsibility to use our talents. God's perception of talents is different for the trusting servants. If we use our talents we will reap not only joy now, but even more talents. Jesus is admitting that life is not fair. Some have less than others.

Our souls shout like the man who received only one talent. My call and one talent are to communicate. The master in Jesus' story demanded that each servant use what he had been given. The problem of the one-talent man was not the gift, but the confusion in him showed that he did not understand the master. Equality was never the issue. The master alone distributed his property. He was not dwelling on the return from his property. The amount of the talent, the type of talent, was not the concern of the master.

The problem in our life journey is not our gifts, but how much we know the master. If not, we are frozen in our tracks by fear, anger, manipulation, and comparisons. Comparing himself to others kept his focus on himself.

Perhaps equality is a human idea. We will never be equal. Each soul is unique. Comparisons keep us bound and limited. We are to use what we have been given.

Use what you have, and God will give you the gift of joy. J. K. Rowling, read by millions, was realistic in saying, "It is impossible to live without failing at something, unless you live so cautiously that you might as well not have lived at all, in which case, you fail by default."

Having It All!

Having all the plethora of being well-positioned reveals the high-achieving woman knows how to live a successful and sensual relationship with ourselves. Creating an atmosphere for joy, she protects her space. She defends her radiance and energy. These are more valuable than time itself. She is her best self, honoring her royalty within.

God loves us unconditionally even if we fail to act joyfully with our perceived burdens. Joy takes root wherever it is planted. Accepting the will of God despite circumstances frees us to bloom where we have been planted. Joy bubbles from knowing that life is filled with talents that can change the world. Living in the days of the German Third Reich, Anne Frank said, "Everyone has inside of her a piece of good news. The good news is that you do not know how great you can be. How much you can love. What you can accomplish and what your potential is."

Joy does not depend on life giving you five talents. Relax. Understand. Be surprised. Be in joy where you are. Blessings unexpectedly flow into your soul.

Trusting God requires accepting who we are. See life itself as God's purpose. Allow difficulties to result in blessings. Joy is our love opening doors for us to use our potential.

There must be a healthy balance between reason and emotion. Unhealthy reason is lifeless, rigid, controlling and compulsive. Healthy emotions yield richer relationships to the texture of life with sunshine, laughter, tears, enthusiasm, along with sadness and pain.

With the world's walls we realize that reason is farsighted, and emotions are nearsighted. Reason can delay satisfaction. Emotions insist on instant gratification.

Emotions are neutral. The become healthy or unhealthy. Out of balance reason and emotion can freeze you. Pity and joy cannot occupy the same soul.

Today there are more women working in traditionally male jobs such as lawyers, physicians, and church senior ministers. Women now serve powerful political, religious, and positions of all types in the free world than ever in the history of human civilization.

Women are serving as queens and presidents bring joy to the world that is ever changing. Feminine wisdom and spiritual power are now overcoming all the discouragement women have endured.

We celebrated the funeral of an 80-year-old woman. Her children, grandchildren and great grandchildren were sitting inside the packed church. She had lived a faithful life and had served the world with humility. God is more pleased with weak but humble virtue than with strong virtue.

Eternal joy in heaven has been prepared. There are no limits. We can all become heroes. Today is not the end of progress. In every age and generation, the cycle of failure and beginning again involves us all. We have failed so many times. Let the masculine and feminine energies be constant in rising again.

Eternal joy is the only emotion we need to express ourselves in heaven. We need to major on the joy of salvation. Joy will free us all. Read John 8:32, II Corinthians 3:17, James 2:12.

Our culture has been marked for the past few centuries by a strong aspiration for freedom. The concept of freedom is often ambiguous. False concepts of freedom and joy alienate people and cause millions of deaths. The desire for freedom and for eternal joy remains active. Despite all the progress made so far, this desire remains. We remain totalitarian. No one can tell us what we must do. Unvaccinated people are dying, because they refuse what could keep them alive.

Aspiration for freedom includes a large dose of illusion and it is fulfilled in mistaken ways. Human beings were not created to live in slavery. We were not created for narrow constricted lives, but we are to live in wide open spaces.

Our great thirst for joy reveals a fundamental aspiration for happiness. There can be no happiness without love. Balancing the masculine and feminine comes as we find joy in loving and being loved.

The problem is that our love goes in wrong directions. We love selfishly and find instead of unconditional love, an atmosphere filled with frustration. If everything that makes us joyless and forever dissatisfied were to mysteriously go away, there might still be limitations and boundaries. Humans want to go farther, faster, and to have a greater power to transform reality.

Feminine power or "being lady -like," cause women to feel like a queen with the whole world at her feet. She has the freedom to travel anywhere on the globe. We want to have a choice in all our circumstances. We desire a choice of jobs, choice in the number of our children, or where we want to go and do. Fundamental aspects of our lives cannot be chosen. Sex. Parents. Eye color. Language. The things we choose in life are not as important than those we have no choice in. The older we get, the fewer options there are for us. Read John 21:18.

How easy it is to go along with situations that are not our choice. We become unpleasant, angry, full of strife and bitterness. We feel a natural revulsion for situations we cannot control. Joy is not bought or conjured up. It comes as a surprise, something we were not looking for.

Renewal requires preparation, transformation, and readiness. We will find expected resistance from many quarters of society. Some are predictable. Some come as a surprise. The word transformation is like conversion, repentance, and changing from one form to another.

We say trans-portation meaning to change locations. Transition means changing states. Change is difficult. Frightening. Unimaginable. Struck down. Wounded. Crushed. Punished. Oppressed. There is nothing easy about the process of transformation.

Joy-bringers fly in the face of patriotism in the most difficult times. Truth means brutal resistance. Transformation generates opposition. We must be prepared to take this step in an atmosphere of opposition. Individuals spearhead transformation. So do communities.

Balancing the masculine and feminine souls brings a rich synergy. Transformation through a network of relationships characterized an inauspicious inconspicuous town in French in *Chocolat*. It happened in a short time when Vianne came to the town.

The joy of chocolate met the spiritual challenges for changing minds. Comte feels guilt and shame for this wife leaving him. He looks for blame and shame in other situations. The free and easy Vianne reminds him of his wife. Comte has economic power over the villagers.

Like some members of a church board or authority, he insists on correcting the pastor's sermons, and he keeps giving examples of how the previous priest did his work to intimidate him. Sounds familiar to me. What about you dear reader?

Pere Henri eventually seizes the opportunity to preach what he wants to preach with the support of his transformation, partly due to Vianne.

Healing the soul of Comte requires him to acknowledge the danger of his control. His wife would never come back. His conversion is shown by his attendance at Vianne's festival.

Men are clueless why women are upset. Women declare that men just don't get it. Masculine and feminine souls communicate with differing reasons. Men need information. Women need an experience for connection. We are uniquely different. It is of interest to a feminine soul to find the details. Men only want facts. Being upset ends when the problem is solved. Upset for women ends when she is fully heard. When I lived in Oxford, there was a picture of Elizabeth I, queen of England. Under it was the quote from her: "I have the heart of a man, not a woman, and I am not afraid of anything."

The gumption of assumption

Alan Alda told us not to assume anything, "Begin challenging your own assumptions. Your assumptions are your windows on the world. Scrub them off occasionally, or the light will not come in." To balance our masculine and feminine sides, do not assume anything. We do learn from each other. Sharing our own stories is cathartic. It helps men and women in their transformation. The only way we can make it through these difficult circumstances is by looking to the examples of others to gain strength and courage. Do not assume anything. Listen closely to each one's story. Offer insight into your own struggles when they are important to understand the issue. Anne Frank wisely noted, "How wonderful it is that nobody need wait a single moment before starting to improve the world."

Be careful to not jump to conclusions. There are two sides to every story. As we hear stories, we make sure we are hearing the whole story. During my ministry, I have observed the expression of the truth from liberal and conservative sides which are unbending.

Our need is to see each other as sacred and need to ignore walls of protection. We need authentic seeing. We do not need more rules. Our voices need to blend for authentic solutions. Together we must be committed to creating a safe sacred space for connection. We need creative spaces for authentic intimate communication. We must be committed to heal the divide and reuniting the masculine and feminine. Israel's leader Golda Meir said, "Whether women are better than men, I cannot say, but I can say they are certainly no worse."

May Becker spoke of human metamorphosis, "We grow neither better nor worse as we get older, but more like ourselves." Sometimes we do not feel like we have the power to be. In times of great change, we will pray that the problems will be opportunities to feel more like ourselves, as we are destined to be.

Peter Marshall, pastor for New York Avenue Presbyterian Church in Washington, spoke of how we together can make life happen: "Let us not be content to wait and see what will happen, but give us the determination to make the right thing happen."

Women are finding their genius. They are believing in their superpower. They act like nobility. Women are decluttering their wardrobes. They discard everything that hides their light and beauty.

They have discovered the power of their sexual energy. They connect the joy of self-love with moments of self-pleasuring. It is so sad that feminine sexual energy in the past has created feelings of disgust or shame, naughtiness, or of something hidden. Using sexual energy has been less than satisfying. God's female children have been harmed mentally, physically, emotionally, and spiritually.

These self-doubts, past relationships, traumas, and limiting beliefs have impacted the energy field. Women who are attracted to men want more and more to walk side by side in a life adventure as they transform into the person they wish to become. She makes good and right choices to live out her purpose and to leave a legacy. She knows how to delight all her senses. She has created a space for self-worth.

"God needed women for survival," Rachel Held Evans said. Jeff Chu, who was in seminary when Held died at 37, edited her thoughts in *Wholehearted Faith*. She writes her thoughts with passionate fire. "And fire," she wrote, "for all its fearsomeness in scripture, can heal, cauterize, and save. Like the seeds that do not sprout without wildfire, new creation cannot come without a good burn." (Rachel Held Evans, ed. Jeff Chu, *Wholehearted Faith*, pp. 20)

Chapter Two

Understanding Joy

For more than 50 years, I have sought to understand joy. The French word "jouissance," meaning highest joy, is both a feminine and a masculine word.

The Hebrew word for joy refers to soaring with gladness. Joy is the human spirit stretching to the limits, burst out of the confines of the wall of the world, eternally dancing through our new human passages. Read Isaiah 12:3.

"There is a revolution in the life cycle. The life cycle has been altered." Gail Sheehy, *New Passages: Mapping Your Life Across Time*, pp. 33-35. Sheehy planned to write a sequel to her first book, but she discovered a historic revolution. This book has uncovered where we are, but she inspires us to make the most of undiscovered territory.

Women and men are discovering entangled webs in their quest for experiencing joy in these complex times. We are missing the joy of salvation. Joy is our resource to create and experience renewing life. We are embraced in the love of God despite the opinions of differing religions, political parties, or any other expressions. Problems and suffering have different meanings. My own journey to understanding joy. I see that part of my purpose to enable people to increase joyous experiences.

I noticed many years ago that all of us are navigating our way through a difficult life situation. Being a human is not easy. My platform of minister of joy is the culmination of my rigorous journey through eight decades. Healing the male soul is to restore our brokenness by God's grace.

Growing old is not living so many years. Freshness comes from not being trapped by negative thinking. Years bring wrinkles to our skin. Our gift from God is who we are. Our gift to God is what we become.

The gist of joy

Joy is contagious. When we remain joyful, whatever circumstances we face, we are acting in a loving way toward the world around us. My wife Laurel often encourages me by saying that we never know the number of people who can be touched by one person. Joy oozes out of use wherever we may be.

J.R. Miller wrote: "Christ is building his kingdom with earth's broken things. Heaven is filling with earth's broken lives, and there is no bruised reed that Christ cannot take and restore to glorious blessedness and beauty. He can take the life crushed by pain or sorrow and make it into a harp whose music shall be all praise. He can lift earth's saddest failure up to heaven's glory."

Faith asks us to accept that God is always at work even if we cannot see it. Restoration can't begin until a problem is fully faced. My friend and joy enhancing fellow writer, Joy Lenton, wrote in Poetry Joy her own dynamics of restoration.

"I'm depleted
Come fall on me like rain
Saturate this place
Shower me with your love
Water all who thirst on earth

I'm sorrowful
Come light my way with joy
I lift my face
Expectant of your goodness
Hungry for your gift of grace

I'm empty
Come fill me to the brim
To overflowing
With an excess to share with a fullness within

I'm worried
Come soothe away the cares
Take the burdens
Lift them from my weary frame
Help me find relief in prayer

I'm praising
Come rejoice and celebrate
My heart ached
God gave me rest and peace
Now god's child has her soul eased

(Joy Lenton, *Poetry Joy*, used by permission)

Read Psalm 72:6. Renewed reassurance of our restless souls comes in times of God's choosing. If we are still digging around in yesterday's detritus, meandering in its mess, we cannot see and sense the presence of God in the here and now. Joy comes dressed as dreams come true. We begin to flourish as our hopes become renewed.

This book can be your steppingstone to balanced awareness. One of my goals is to present to my readers how interconnected we are to the world through relationships.

A Vision Quest for Joy Is Revolution

We have our work cut out for us on the days when light and joy are absent. All souls feel downcast, we need deliberate efforts to stay encouraged to pursue joy.
We live in a fallen world that drains every ounce of our energy.

An inner revolution is happening. The world's walls are breaking. When you fight to find joy, when you attempt to smile. The good and positive is not out of reach. There are no easy answers. There are no easy problems. Only possibilities and choices. We cannot teach what we do not understand. We cannot understand what we do not explore and study.

Men who participated in a vision quest summarized what it meant to them. A vision quest is a communion with spirit, a shedding of the old. A journey. An adventure. A guiding. A dying and rebirth. A transition with spirit. A return realizing internal changes. A meeting with your real self. A seeking beyond ordinary sight. A rite of passage. A severance from daily life. A cry for a vision.

I take lots of photographs of places and times of joy. I rush to call and describe it to my loved ones. Joy is a social thing. Lauren Bacall saw life as a roller coaster, "As for the future, I will go on believing there is one that is full of joy. This adventure is not over." Our life journey is an amazing adventure. Life's ups and downs make living an interesting experience. The joy of the Lord gives us strength to endure and never to give in. Life happens in a rhythm like a roller coaster. George Bernard Shaw lived life to the max saying, "You cannot learn to skate without being ridiculous. The ice of life is slippery."

When my time on earth ends, I want to be splattered from head to toe as I kick the last ball trough the goalposts. I want to know and feel where I have been and the joys I felt. The closer to my time to leave, the more I realize what I do not know. Each day I find topics tat I know nothing about. There is always something more to learn. This invigorates life.

Finding Joy in Transformation

Thousands of people who have shared their joy experiences with me collaborates the joy beyond the walls of this world. Joy is experienced in a variety of ways. It may be described as a time of intense happiness. Finding joy does not come from the world's demand for external stimulation.

Story tellers such as C.S. Lewis and Tolkien use the word *eucatastrophe*. The word means God's restoring the world to what it is meant to be. What a positive twist to the writing concerning the Apocalypse! Humans will be transformed in impossible ways. Humans will no longer oppress the weakest. We will live in harmony with each other. Destruction, death, and misunderstanding will cease.

The reward will be a life filled with joy. Receiving blessings does not depend on what we have done in the past. Blessings come in the present. In the joyful now, we keep smiling, no matter what a day is like. Mark Twain wrote, "On with the dance, let joy be unconfined whether there's any dance to dance or any joy to unconfine."

With my more than half a century of ministry and clinical psychotherapy work, the existence of joy in the human spirit has transformed all that I do. Joy is more than contentment. It is the delight of each day of our living. Joy is the natural capacity for intense, volitional elation. Joy is transcendence of the soul to a higher level. A patient at the mental hospital where I served as a psychiatric therapist came to hear me preach a few years after her recovery and dismissal from the hospital. I had used a different approach to understanding her behavior. We examined what she was doing right rather than when she was wrong. She had every right to hate the world, but instead she came to love her existence. We unearthed her joys and her family enjoyed her rather than just attempting to cope with her.

As minister of joy to the world, everything involving joy communication brings new possibilities. Joy-filled people break free from traditional limits. The lead lives of more choice and freedom. Being free in this now moment is what I am trying to communicate.

Open your heart. Open your eyes. Go outside this world's walls. Research on joy has been sparse. People want to know what joy is. Before you read on, sit quietly in a comfortable place, and think about the most joyful moment of your life. Smile as you absorb your feeling and picture of that wonderful time and visualize making that joy a part of everyday.

Intense emotion and experience are too much for mere words. Joy is difficult to verbalize. I have collected thousands of individual's attempts to find words to share what their unique joy experience is like. Joy is the most intimate of human experience. Expressing joy is to reveal what is right for you.

Joy is a way to know this world. This new way is an intuitive one. Surprisingly, joy is beyond the walls of logic and reasoning. Joy brings appreciation, even amazement. Appreciate the simple things. When I shared the time my daughter and I looked deeply into each other's blue eyes. Her eyes sent out a light. Joy is a complete realization of the simple aspects of our living.

Relationships are like a mirror all cleaned up. We must not see only pain and unresolved challenges. When we relate to another person, we see a reflection of something that is within us. Because we see joy in our relationships, we share their joy.

Any crisis gets challenging when we see in the mirror anger, protectiveness, or distance, jealousy, frustration, and even hate. We call each other incompetent, inconsiderate, rude, and disconnected. Whatever it is that you judge in another person hat cause you to be angry, hurt, frustrated, annoyed, or sad shows up in some way inside of you.

Our workplaces, our churches, places within our current culture ae reinforcing men that there is a masculine wrongness, disrespect if they reach out and touch women. Any touch or contact is interpreted as inappropriate and unwanted. Institutions today fear lawsuits or wrath or loss of jobs or power.

We resist the feeling of a group of people cuddled in for a photograph. Putting an arm around a shoulder, a hand placed on a hand, or a clergy photo with men and women displayed in ways that do not fit denominational agenda.

Men have to second guess their words and actions. Some are embarrassed o ashamed that they are men. Men are to be blamed. Women think they must control and manage lives, or everything will fall apart. These sad truths do not need to continue. It is still possible to heal the division.

Joy connects us with each other.

That is how we connect with each other. Joy eludes us as we grow further apart. To know surprising joy, we must take risks. These joy risks are not impossible or dangerous things. Joy requires courage.

When anyone shares a joy, their report contains a soteriological sense of being born again. When a person appears younger than their years of age, the reason is explained by the ageless joy with which they choose to live. Joy revives the soul.

One can cross lines of definition. We tend to look outside ourselves for solutions for which we refuse to take responsibility. Society and culture are really nothing. People within society are society. Looking without gets into impossible expectation. When we expect a certain level of performance from other humans, we shall be disappointed. Transformation is not found in where we are going, but in how we handle the journey. Life is what happens while we are planning. Life does not happen out there. It happens within.

Men do not have a rite of passage. Perhaps this is the root of our male identity crisis. If we are to choose a process to experience, it would come from other cultures such as the native American. They called this a Vision Quest. It became a passage for conversion, acceptance, and a change of energy from the male feminine existence to the masculine responsibility-oriented existence.

This passage blends feminine receptivity into masculine aggression or assertion energy. It is natural for men to use the right brain to create a life vision. Life becomes exciting, passionate, and productive. I am not suggesting that men go on a Native American vision quest. We can adapt versions that help men know themselves. Details of a vision quest varies from tribe to tribe.

Scripture tells of the vision quests of Abraham, Isaac, and Jacob, as well as that of Jesus. The intention was spiritual as well as practical giving the gift of joy for masculine living. During my weekend retreats called Visionquests for Joy, men as well as women find this a profound and rewarding experience.

Survival of future generations will require a new and fresh look at energy forces. A Vision Quest opens us up to living daily from and for a vision.

If you find a particular man with whom you feel a mentoring relationship appropriate, explore it because of mutual benefit. It is quite possible that it will be an exciting and lesion-filled adventure. You will grow and expand your soul. Be kind and loving and the other person will need to understand and be willing to share the experience. This inner work is never easy. Men are not accustomed to these kinds of relationships with other men.

My best supervisor at Valley Hope was an engaging black man. Joe often said, "Healing unlocks the joy held captive inside our souls." Little has changed since the Civil Rights Movement as to the transformation of our race relationships. Others move on with their lives. They must accept the world we live in. We are amazed at the joy of our black brothers and sisters. Many, like Joe, know that they have a choice to find happiness and joy rather than spending their lives in misery.

Black women and men deserve joy. The walled in world for black people has magnified black anger more than anything. My black women friends have shared with me the infamous "angry black woman" that originated from past generations. Their shared stories suggested that all black women are sassy, hostile, and aggressive. An attractive black woman said, "People think only blue-eyed blondes are beautiful. They reveal their racism. I know that is an unfair assessment of black women."

I have served as pastor of lack churches, taught at black schools and seminaries, and ministered through psychotherapy with black families in black neighborhoods. These experiences have shown me that black women are not a monolith. They come from differing walks of life. When a black woman finds healing, it unlocks all the joy that has been held captive inside.

We need black joy especially in these times of stress and rapid change because it promotes the survival of all people. Black joy disrupts pain and saves us. Joy is proactive. Black joy surprises us as black individuals experience life in the simplest pleasures. I'm impressed by black women's imagination. They do not need to earn the right to experience joy. Black women and black men need to unapologetically immerse themselves in whatever brings them joy.

Joy is the birthright of all people. Just like their demands for justice, the joy must not be negotiable. Joy is the key spiritual gift for freedom. Without joy, nobody can be free. As my terrific administrative director said, "Conversion to God and my transformation is holding the hand of the little girl inside of me. I want her to know how much I love her. I will never stop looking for ways to multiply her joy. Being a black woman in and of itself brings joy.

Black Women are the most mistreated people in the United States.

Black women enjoy hanging out with other black women. They can organize a book club. They can give each other foot massages and facials. Simple things have always brought them joy.

Joy is the knowledge that you can fulfill your dreams. You can never fulfill the false expectations of society's view of your potential. Joy does not have to be earned. It is a natural human right. Joy is not achieved. Joy is received. Joy is within you. It does not need to be defended. Men and women share today's uncomfortable crisis.

Living in the joy of retirement

When I retired my fellow retiree noted that retirement means having and taking time to enjoy life abundantly. We should consider retiring throughout life. The assumption is that we'll have time "later" after working hard enough and long enough, we will be rewarded.

Retirement might bring chronic illness, loss of opportunity, rejection, and power.

We might be forced to live a long distance from our family, struggling to contact others. We must live our lives now in the prime times for joy.

The joy of living is bound up in how joy surprises us. When our female and masculine energies are properly balanced, surprises are the fuel of the power fire within us.

Joy needs human connection.

Joy comes on the physical level when we hold, touch, and hug each other. Most of us could not live in complete isolation. We do not want to accept the wall that Robert Frost said to tear down. Joy needs human connection. We learn from others. Find someone to share a new project such as starting a hobby, learning to dance, to beat on drums in rhythms.

Society connects external intensity with degree of closeness and attention. We will not take the time to know the world as it is until we take down the isolation walls. Joy is being in tune with the flow of life. The joy response is connecting, joining with somebody else. All disease is a form of disconnection. Our need is to spark connection to all people by thinking and behaving in ways that consider the welfare of others, but to give others an equal billing with you. We behave from an instinctual understanding about the care of each member the world and the wellbeing of everyone as the whole creation.

Human connection and joy must be enlisted in finding other people who share your goals. That connection is the ultimate gift we give to ourselves. If our culture continues to divide into a connection of untouchables and human touchable folks, the walled-up world can again find connection and soul touch.

When we laugh and smile connects us with other's joy. As we enjoy the joy that they experience, our own joy emerges. For joy and love, we are required to relearn acceptance to the present moment. We must learn to live nonjudgmentally, with acceptance and forbearance. We can not afford to attach ourselves to the future at the expense of now. Joy brings congeniality. Consonance. Accord. Compassion. These are areas at the base of tolerance. Being rational, responsive, responsible, and respectful are the keys. With these we can welcome change and anticipate that our rapid changes will bring out our ability to cope as change occurs.

Joy is the source of the light we are seeking. Joy brings an enduring self-esteem, confidence, faith, and the belief that things will tourn out for our good because all of us are connected for and by our common journey's ultimate purpose.

Some will do anything to be on good terms by relating to people of power. By doing that we let it be known that we are special. We think we are superior if we link ourselves to authority. This is the picture of fabricated feelings of superiority.

Inferiority is the real base for these actions. Unhappy people keep repeating, "You do not understand how I feel." Completely understanding the feelings of a person who feels rejected is something no person can do. There is no need for comparing oneself with another.

Joy is like a collage or a tapestry. Joy blends disjointed division into a whole. Joy transforms us to call every nation our own, to call every women part of the family. We never get into a joy time with a clenched fist.

Joy begins with a commitment. The contract brings an awareness that you were created capable of happiness and health in every season of life. Make a personal promise that you will accept responsibility for using your gift of joy. The dominance of the male or yang in living can crowd out the yin or feminine side.

That yin and yang balance goes far beyond the social roles of women and men.

Femininity brings intuition. It is an essential wisdom. Our world will spin even further from its foundation without it.

The yang in us represents analytic, controlling, rational orientation. A "woman's movement" can be as dangerous as a "man's movement." We are required to integrate each side. We create our experiences through our hopes, our perceptions, and our interpretation of how the world turns. A culture is defined s a symbiotic system. "Culture" is a term from the Latin language" word *colere*. It means to tend to the earth. The word is linked to the concept of nurturing. My Latin teachers at Tennessee High School and Carson-

Newman would enjoy knowing that I have used my Latin studies. We learn a lot from this now dead language. Latin was the language used by the Catholic church because a dead language never changes.

Nothing is separate. Everything is linked together. Every choice we make touches everything, everywhere, and the choices we made determine the future.

Deep Needs for Identity

Humans possess a deep need for identity. We need to exist in our own eyes and in the eyes of others. At the most superficial levels, the need for identity seeks satisfaction in material possessions. Realizing that the only thing others were interested in was the money, not themselves. When a human being loses her or his memory, health, talents or abilities, they lose identity behind the walls of this world. The joy of getting to use out talents brings self-confidence and the urge to trust the will of God and the reality of life. Society gives a unique value and dignity to people with high aptitudes. We cultivate a self that is different from our real self. Large amounts of human energy are needed to maintain an artificial self.

Love brings trust. Trust beings joy. God gives us roots to hold us upright as we experience our life journey. Seeing each moment as a love gift frees our souls to soar with enthusiasm. Some decisions made by superiors causes one to cease with their talents. This brings on profound crisis to the point that one has no identity.

We possess the blessing of being alive. God uses our limitations and failures as the means to be who we are and where we are. Our earthly journey is brief. Nobody's trip ends where she or he expected it to end when the trip first began.

Disappointments and failures are seen as unendurable. They are perceived as an attack on our being. The dark night of the soul comes with impoverishments, violence, unending swift changes that strip us from ever relying on ourselves. God love us unconditionally with immense grace. God makes use of our every experience to help us in our transformation with joy. Our only support and tenderness found in the mercy of God. Support is from God alone.

Many life experiences cause perplexity. Intense darkness surrounds us during our life journeys. Things can cause your soul to appear frozen. The joy of the Lord will be your strength. As we discover ourselves and that no external source can take away our joy.

Joy surprises us when we are not wrapped inside ourselves. Selflessness is the key. My own life has been blessed with joy, but none so beautiful s when I give my self and all my gifts and graces to other people. Belonging to a place is entirely different from owning a place. When you belong to your family, community, or church, you are in a relationship with everything and everybody in the universe. Being in relationship requires attention.

Attention brings familiarity. Familiarity grows into intimacy. Intimacy elicits a human urge to join with others to protect and care for the places we love.

People of joy are not troubled by their weaknesses. They never blame other people for not always meeting their expectations. They desire nothing. They are not living in fear of anything. We cannot know or predict what will happen in the third millennium. Only those who have discovered the inalienable space of freedom that God has placed inside their souls by created them as children, will never be caught off guard. Overwhelming joy is part of our lives. Joy is our connection to other human beings. Joy does not happen in a vacuum. We always feel connecting to those who live beyond the walls of the world.

Any writing or conversation is like a web. It connects our thoughts on racism education, healthcare, housing, minimum wage, burnout, incarceration, voter suppression. Each topic affects and is affected by the rest.

Stimulating conversation brings truth into the light. The need to be right is a big bar to new thoughts. My friends—both introverts and extraverts, men and women, clergy and laypersons are all big talkers who love keeping up with what is going on. Conversation is stimulating and scintillating, and sometimes by a miracle some opinions are turned completely around. People who are filled wit the Spirit of joy respect and care for each other.

Any conversation about human relationships cannot be unraveled from the ways we treat each other and the ways we treat the universe.

The Good News is joy for the uncounted, the unacceptable, the unwanted, the problems, the masses living in terror and fear. In joy, we learn to pity others. We try to love as the world continues to experience political events, personal griefs, and violence. We listen Attend. Give time. Offer friendship. Encourage. Hope. Pool resources. Connect.

One of my favorite Christian writers is Frederick Buechner, an inspirational writer, who is an ordained Presbyterian (USA) minister whose writing has been the bulk of his ministry. He received a transformation in his life while a member of the Madison Avenue Presbyterian Church in New York City.

I was given a plaque from the Pilgrim Presbyterian Church in Cameron, Missouri for about ten years. It was labeled,

"The Great Dance." I think these words are appropriate the share with my readers now.

"Joy is home. God created us in joy and created us for joy, and in the long run not all the darkness there is in the world and in ourselves can separate us from that joy, because whatever else it means to say that God created us in his image, I think it means that even when we cannot believe in God, even when we feel most spiritually bankrupt and deserted by him, his mark in deep within us. We have God's joy in our blood." (Frederick Buechner, "The Great Dance," *Secrets in the Dark: A Life of Sermons*)

Chapter Three

Surrendering for Joy

Surrender is not a positive term for most men. Men hate quitters. Quitting. Giving up. Conceding. Stopping. Failing. What is a virtue to some is a disaster to others. Faith is never at odds with science. Social scientists agree that the fundamental needs of humans is to become part of something transcendent. Men and women seek joy that lies beyond pain and pleasure. Secular researchers prove to women and men that faithful people are happier, have more satisfaction and joy.

What prevents you from surrendering yourself completely to God?

The process of surrender allows the past to be done and the future to become. To save us from male toxification we must let go of beliefs and the systems that hold us back from fulfilling our potential. We are responsible to make the changes for redeeming the world. Let go of trying to be right or correct. Release the pain, the endless arguments, ego conflict, and disappointment. Surrender the lie that you can have it all. Surrender to love. Create newness with love. Make every life choice in love. Never expect perfection. There are no easy joy rides. Nothing different can happen if we do not surrender to doing life differently.

Life moves slowly for a long time, and nothing happens until the eggshell cracks, the branch blossoms, the tadpole's tail shrinks away, the leaf falls. Every transformation begins with an ending. We must surrender the old thing before picking up the new thing.

In Lewis Carroll's classic, written when he served as a mathematics professor at the University of Oxford, Alice says, "At least I knew who I am when I got up this morning, but I think I must have changed several times since then." (Lewis Carroll, *Alice's Adventures in Wonderland*, p. 47)

Giving Up Is Giving Out

When we surrender or give up things, we also are giving out. If we decide to others, it involves some things you would like to keep yourself. If we give money to charity involves not getting to spend money on something you wanted for yourself. Surrender creature comforts and personal security are surrendered.

Surrender to the integration of masculine and feminine energy. We are not writing about gender when it comes to life energy. Embrace that male and female energy are within us all. Because of the past conditioning from culture, we need help to balance these energies. Type A people demonstrate too much masculine energy.

Balance of male and female energies leads to wholeness, peace, and satisfaction.

These energies are within, and joy comes as they are integrated. This integration benefits everyone. We shall enjoy feeling lighter and more energized and more loved in our relationships. This takes effort and practice. It results in connection with our true and authentic selves. Choose to nourish your own soul. Honor the integrity of yourself and others, your community, and all of life.

Shame and loathing are difficult paths. Visualize your sustainable, holistic, reconstructed, transformed masculinity for men. And for women. Guilt because of the past hangs over our heads like a heavy weight. Guilt gnaws on our inner souls like a swarm of termites on pieces of wood. We must let go of some self-images and styles of coping.

Our addictions to routine, security, and comfort causes us to become unable to meet some challenges. "Real change will come when powerful women are less of an exception. It is easy to dislike senior women because there are so few." Sheryl Sandberg said these words. Progress is never swift or easy.

Both genders must realize that interbeing and inter dependency are organic for all humans. Work environments have held traditional masculine traits. With this limited and limiting imagination, masculinity has become a lonely place. I cannot count the number of coaching or counseling sessions I have had with men who are adjusting to the new economy and fear of the direction of feminine power.

Joy comes as people that I have encountered, both men and women, involve transformation through a conversional encounter with a Higher Power. They have been as C.S. Lewis said, "surprised by joy." The surrendered life means we are never alone in any circumstance or how changes affect the world.

Only God deserves absolute surrender. Only God offers dependable love. This surrender need not be threatening for God is the epitome of love and goodness. Joy, not fear, brings us into an authentic relationship.

Relationship-centered prayer brings energies toward life as it should be, on earth as it is in heaven. Strong women that I have known became even stronger through worship.

Surrender is not an either-or affair. Women and men must gain the knowledge of who they are. It is much easier to lose sight of who we are when things are going well for us than when we realize a crisis and live under stress. The Bible says it well. Read Philippians 4:11-12.

Our wounded souls are wary because being loved and loving others is not easy. We automatically keep the walls of the world as barriers and defenses of our discontentment. Those barriers built up over time must be broken down. We must love ourselves in a balanced way. Panic has gripped us far too long.

No matter how many friends you have, it is difficult to be content unless we learn to befriend ourselves, acknowledge our hurt, pain, mistakes and ways we have missed the mark in loving ourselves who each of us really is.

Open your eyes. See that life is more than tasks. Life is not just success, but life acknowledges weaknesses. We know our small part matters. Laura Colson tells of her confirmation by going through almost every situation a woman could imagine. (Lara Colson, *Restore the Joy: A Transformation Through Confirmation*, pp. 1-138)

Colson describes a genuine transparency about the trials and triumphs of her personal life. Being poor, black, female, divorced, a life-threatening medical diagnosis, her book includes feminine insight and inspiration.

Balance is necessary for harmony.

Colson has reminded us that balance is necessary for harmony. Lisa Miller is a neuroscientist who studies innate spirituality. Her research cites soul surrendering for experiencing joy, love, connection, and unity. This transformation makes us increase resilience and lowers rates of depression. Surrendering our baggage causes us to become fully aware of a transcendent higher power. "What is good for everyone is also what is best for each one of us,"

Miller writes. (Lisa Miller, *Christian Century*, September 22, 2021, p. 8)

Confusion reigns in everything we do. Life endings bring on disengagement. Distant identification. Disenchantment. Disorientation. If I had been fully aware of the atmosphere in churches that bring hate, division, and pains, I would not have given so much energy, time, and money to become a pastor. We believe the lies that are glamorized and told to us. Perhaps our current church situation may not be as sinister as lying. Lying is an action of intentional misrepresentation of what is the reality. Some people who have never been appointed or called to serve as pastors feel compelled to speak without knowing what they are talking about. Being prepared for the unexpected requires being prepared to be unprepared. Replace fear with grace. Love while we still exist. When we travel our earthly journey, we realize that our thoughts, our sexuality, our gender, our race, our humility is often used as a license to harm us.

Liars misrepresent truth on purpose. We need to be part of the solution and bring things into the light. Our beautiful gift of femininity is our pearl of great price. We can tie our pearls together. Wrap the pearls in forgiveness around your problems that may have resulted from lies from the father of lies. The women God has called to bring the chosen people into the world were ordinary women who struggled with every problem that blocked their path.

Let us join to become closer to God who is in love with all of us. Read Genesis 2:22. That was in the beginning. We are starting our own beginning in the rapidly changing world now. When God created everything from nothing, God choose to create us. God knit us together in our mother's womb. We were made intentionally, not by accident. Homo sapiens are different. That difference lies beyond our chromosomes and physical attributes. That creation is as deep as our souls. Expressions of humanity differs in the ways we love, how we think, how we function and connect. Men and women are equal, and each is filled with dignity.

Like Carroll's words of Alice, we bring the "me" of the day. Some days we feel peaceful. Other days we are stormy and dark. Our minds may be racing. Our inner being is unsettled. We bring our worries and discontentment in a huge backpack. Reflect on Psalm 139:1-2. Everything is temporary.

Here I am. Small but empowering words. We come in our spiritual sloppiness and say, "Here I am." God knows us better than we know ourselves. God uses simple people to accomplish amazing things. Women with men touch the world. It has nothing to do with one person being more special. It is the grace of God. Quiet your soul and ask for the grace you need for today. Do not worry about the future.

Written into the female soul is the desire to be pursued and protected. Letting a man open a door for you, cooking dinner, carrying a heavy package does not subtract from a woman's strength. Surrender is not about being passive. Surrendering is like a tug of war. Gender battles inevitable come in some type of power struggle. Women go from giving themselves completely to a relationship to the messy work involved in establishing a sense of balance and equilibrium.

This balancing is necessary for the stability and security within a relationship that secures trust. The root of these power struggles is believing you are right, and your friend or partner is wrong. Not surrendering to being passive is the first step toward gaining clarity and resolution.

Life is not all about happy endings. It is about joyful, wondrous moments in between frightening moments in between tedious moments. In between surprising and ecstatic times. Within this spiral, where is the ending?

Surrender the tendency for control and shift from what we can get to what can I give. The question that propels our rich earthly existence is, "What can we achieve together?" More men are finding surrender, rather than submission. To receive a more pleasurable relationship, surrender narrows the masculine-feminine gap.

Both genders flourish and self-fulfillment is perceived as significant.

Each of us carry more creativity than we are aware of, along with feistiness, ingenuity, tenacity and power. Will we surrender our false selves enough to trust each other before it is too late? Our ancestors living thousands of eras ago understood that cooperation was required if humans were to survive.

Transformation is about risk. It is about letting go and giving what we have for other people's needs. It is sharing and being the first to move toward others. Conversion brings generosity. It means blessing our gifts. It is remembering to pick up the leftovers, so nothing is wasted. Transformation involves surrendering our personal agenda to help those in worse condition than we are.

Surrendering for joy is to speak to the many lacking things in our current world.

Lack of bread. Lack of resources. Lack of direction. Lack of worship. Lack of spirit. Lack of trust. Lack of joy. Intimacy with Jesus starts with forgetting ourselves. Strangers like the chocolate maker in *Chocolat* have needs that we can meet and receive. She fed people her chocolates even as she observes their mischief. Meeting the needs of those who have a lack is sweet surrender.

This is where we begin the kingdom of joy. The eternal joy of the Lord is to have taken away from us what we have been given for the use of God. The majority of the people living in this world are not making it.

The Bible is our constitution. People's lives are where we put the Bible into practice. Our practice causes the majority of people not to have to simply endure. Women and children are among those who endure. Even though women are the majority in our churches, in the nation, and in the world, they must be the ones saddled with endurance.

The kingdom will come despite our political systems and our reluctance to change, despite the lacks. Faithful people are required to anticipate needs as Jesus did. The disciples then and today are insensitive to these lacks.

Surrendering brings about miracles that everyone has enough and there is joy in any community with the presence of God. Joy cannot happen until somebody takes a risk. Hugh Wamble, my church history professor at Midwestern Baptist Theological Seminary, took out his translation of the *Didache* and read, "See how Christians love one another."

The body of Christ s offered his bread, and in that gift, we are being offered the whole people as well as the person of Christ. Within a starving community, the is always enough for strangers and taking care of anyone who shows up at the communion table are given joy and hope.

This truth has massive ramifications for our theology and our lives. Inviting all to the table is a radical conversion.

Disciples of Christ are called to learn to chew on the scriptures that we attest to believe and preach. None of us are Christ, but we are Christ-like no matter our gender.

Harriet Martineau said, "You had better live your best and act your best and think your best today; for today is the sure preparation for tomorrow and all the other tomorrows that follow." It is the urgent that matters.

Say yes to the puzzling and joy of the wonder of mutual love. The place where we expect grace the least is where it lives most. Oceans of grace, fountains of grace, rivers of grace, creeks of grace. Waters of grace swirl as we surrender our pride, our complaining, and our stubborn wills.

Surrendered disciples go way beyond compliance. Amazing things happen when we choose to surrender to God. Life is made of choices. Decisions we make today determine our future.

The final line in the New Testament speaks of grace. John ends his visions on the island of Patmos with a blessing that has become a familiar blessing in every crisis in history. The word is spoken in a multitude of languages. "The grace of our Lord Jesus Christ be with you all. Amen.

Chapter Four

Cultivating Joy in Relationships

Scientific research reveals that the brain records and stores within its depths literally 100 per cent of everything we see, hear, or experience. How we react is not created from conscious desire, but from unconscious reaction. We are the cause of all our effects. Joy does not dominate. It cultivates. "Sister is probably the most competitive relationship within the family, but once sisters are grown, it becomes the strongest relationship," observed Margaret Mead.

Transformation of our souls comes from introducing positive possibilities to our conscious awareness, so that reprogramming, repatterning, conversion, occurs with unconditional love. A small minority controls the church because others let them. Churches need relationships t sharpen our awareness that as we gather in the presence of God. Sometimes the dominant minority does not welcome the scruffy prodigals who live within the sight of the steeples of churches.

Cultivating joy comes from a new point of view about others' right to differ from us. Our ability to grow and learn is enhanced by sublimating our desires to new possibilities. Together men surrendering to a false self can be transformed and help save our wounded world. Read John 4:4-26.

To claim we love God but, we continue to harbor prejudice about someone who was created in the image of God. That is crazy. Without taking time to get to know people, all we have left is our assumptions about them, based on cultural stereotypes and partial or wrong information.

Every ethnic group in heaven and on earth is recognized By God. God is able to do far beyond the walls of this world than all we could ask or imagine. Allow people to know your heart. The community we are creating within our congregations that we are called to lead is the same community that you are part of. Integrate yourself as a member of that community. Integrate together, rather than think you are above it.

Jesus was not afraid to interact with men and women from a differing religion or ethic group, or even a female with dubious morals. When we got to close for comfort, the woman in John's account quickly tried to divert him into other general controversy. He was just as quick to turn her thought around to the essence of the matter.

Relationships are important to God. It is impossible to separate our relationship with God from relationships with each other. Read I John 4:19-21.

Followers of Jesus should be more concerned with one another than we are with ourselves. I must fight for you. And you must fight for me. I must stand up for you. You must see that I am cared for. In many congregations, people don't know one another well enough to be able to care for one another. They do not know what each other's needs are to be able to be of support.

Vianne had non-religious roots. She tells her daughter about her grandparents. Put yourself in the place of one without any faith searching for something to believe in and someplace to belong. What would cause you to cultivate a relationship with the marginalized people? We are all quite small in the universe. Some smaller congregations make the mistake that congeniality is a genuine community. That's why we are avoiding controversial topics.

Only decades of vulnerable ministry in local congregations have been the best preparation to continue to share with as many people as possible.

It wasn't until I retired from serving a formal pastorate that a small group met to continue pursuing joy. We meet inside our new home. The authentic metaphor for my humble work is the account of Jesus feeding the multitude. Our gatherings are risky and exciting. The excitement was huge in what we shared in our relationship as a group of folks who no longer wanted to be part of a congregation ruled by a few. The interchange revealed the faith struggles of common people. This Spirit of Joy gathering provided a context for ongoing dialogue in or out of the church.

Relating Is the Soul of Life

Relatedness is an attribute of God. Relating with men and women is important. Read I John 1:3, 1:7; I Corinthians 1:9; Philippians 2:1; Acts 2:42; and I Thessalonians 2:17, 20.

We need intimacy from the day we were born. Infants will die without cuddling. Men and women who have come to me for psychotherapy enlisted my help because of failure to develop relationships.

Joy breaks through the surface of life and shines into the light on all so that we see ourselves for who we really are. This joy is a moment of grace that is mysterious and transcendent. I relate to Serene Jones' theology. Serving as president of Union Seminary, New York, she says that God is in her story. Love, joy, and beauty in in her inner experiences. Jesus is the center of her theology. "Jesus is the truest human being manifestation in life form." God does not stay at a distance. Jesus transforms her life and awakens her to have new eyes. She notes her definition of conversion is "to see anew." Jones has women know that God is walking nearby. God is waiting around the next corner. (Serene Jones, *Call It Grace: Finding Meaning in a Fractured World*, pp. 1-79)

Relating is the source of joy. Relating can also bring pain and sorrow. We take a risk when we establish a family. Children are a blessing from God. The loving adventure of a husband and wife is a source of joy. Two become one and they rejoice. Joy in marriage does not depend on dramatic events. Marital joy occurs in the small everyday living. Joy is an outgrowth or reward of intimate sharing.

Relationships provide meaning and a sense of purpose. Relating brings the feeling of being needed. The worst thing we can do is to stand still with any situation as it is. It is impossible to live completely alone. Humans, including clergy, are inexorably related to sinners, which is all of us. Relating includes joining in repentance. Walking along together, we must turn around, changing our direction, and changing the consequences of sin. We can't undo our sins, but we can undo these sins, but we can undo he damage. For us not to do anything is to reinforce and continue the consequence of sin.

Who we are speaks louder than the words we say or what we do. We need to act quicker to acknowledge differences than to condemn. The circle of relating returns to the beginning in knowing equivocally that nobody has grasp of the truth.

We should try to be wholly ourselves. We are quite unique in how we looked, thought, and related to another. We are not to start over inside our mother's womb. Our place of birth, our parents, our background, or culture. Relating in joy is to experience the world with childlike eyes.

"No single person, however gifted, has led complex social change on her own," says Amy Frykholm in *Christian Century*, September 22, 2021, p. 10.

Men live in hidden struggles. It is difficult for men to reconcile their childhood images of their fathers and most men in their lives. One way of healing is to examine their fathers' histories. Men need to discover ways of being empathetic to his father's pain. The women's movement has provided daughters with a way to understand and forgive their mothers, but we have little sense of our father's journey. Understanding our father's struggle and realizing the broken connection between fathers and sons as part of the unfinished business of masculine living. Many family secrets concerning fathers have to do with a work setback that cripples a father's relationship with his family.

In learning about their fathers, sons realize they are separate people, different from themselves. That speeds up the separation-individualization process. The son sees his responsibility for his own identity as a man who is not chained to the father.

Healing the masculine soul is complex when a father is dead or physically unavailable. It is in those atmospheres that a man is deprived of the actual emotional healing that results from common ground with one's father.

The inner image of my own father is no longer a critical, angry, inferior-feeling one. Transforming my soul has made me more accepting and forgiving. I am cured of any need to be an authoritarian, unyielding figure in my own relationships.

The essential image for healing is the internal image of father and the sense of masculinity that a son carries in his mind and soul. Understanding the poignant reasons why the past was as it was.

We do have a deep need to explore satisfying ways to be male in our unique identity. There is a healthy realization that we are our father's son without accepting and loving everything about him and what happened as we walked our journey together.

Every male needs to identify the good in his father, to know how we are like them, and the ways we are different from them. We gain a fuller sense of the joys of being masculine that results in caring and nurturing, being strong without being negative and destructive.

I have used the following exercise in weekend vision quests. Participants write in a notebook these possibilities.

1. Ten things I would like to have in my life.
2. Ten things I would like to not have in my life.
3. Ten people whom I would like to know I love them.
4. Ten people whom I would like to know love me.
5. Ten reasons why I believe the results I have projected through these questions do not exist in my life now.

Women have less problem completing this exercise. Risk is involved. This is an opportunity to put into writing what you believe you want out of life. Until you find out what you want, nothing is going to happen.

All relationships end. We do not know how or when. Death ends a life, but it does not end a relationship. None of us are ever ready for the full impact of the end of a loving relationship. I coped with my recent parents' and my brother's death by writing a book.

Recognize the unlimited opportunities for enjoying life more frequently. We find joy in difficult circumstances. Joy experiences nurture in relationships and fosters personal growth. Joy enhances the quality of life for everyone.

Under the gaze of God, we are delivered from the constraint of having to be the best. Releasing efforts to show ourselves in a favorable light, e can be what we are. Rest like little children in the joy of our loving God by being what we are. We imagine that our deficiencies make us unlovable. We try to make ourselves face more negativity. We are just not good enough. We are daring to aspire. Women and men are not imprisoned within mediocrity or forced into a dull resignation. Even if we fall every day, we can get up again. We tend to carry around limiting beliefs and unreal convictions that cause us to think we will never be capable of doing what we have envisioned.

We forbid wholesome aspiration, accomplishment, or surprising joy. The call of God comes with sacrifices Nothing stays beyond our reach. People need to accept themselves in order to accept those within our relationships. It is a two-way deep connection. Each one strengthens the others. Not accepting ourselves, we create inner tension. Dissatisfaction and frustration taken out on other people. Being at odds with your colleagues means being at odds with ourselves. There is no joy continuing to be perpetual victims of harsh judgments and narrow heartedness. Our narrow vision needs to be opened to the wisdom of God. That means repentance and renewal.

Those moments of our lives when our minds grasp what God is doing, what God is calling us to do, enables us to cooperate with the work of grace. No soul is a puppet.

Certain ambiguities and needs must be purified. Every human wants to take over, grasp the reins, master the situation, and sense the humbleness of power. Most of us live with insecurity. We seek security so that we can control situations. That security is fragile, human, and deceptive. Full inner freedom results from freeing ourselves from the need for human security through the realization that God alone is our security. For many years Methodists held guaranteed appointments for its elders. Elders are members of a conference in full communion. United Methodist ministers have never decoded the mystery of why all that has recently changed.

Needing to feel security we search for the will of God. Even if one does everything they can with reflection, prayer, and spiritual guidance, she or he will not always get a clear answer. Lacking answers about the future, we must prepare to later receive them by living today to the full anointment of God. Read John 10:18.

Jesus' life was taken from him. He was put in chains, beaten, condemned, and crucified. Jesus accepted what God wanted. Even his death resulted in joy. His life taken became a life given. The joy of God transforms any event in our lives into an expression of love, trust, hope, and surrender. Positive results become the reason for the joy in thanksgiving. Everything can be described as grace. This attitude is neither spontaneous nor normal, but it is the only was to achieve interior peace.

God made us to be differing. Some must love everything in order, those who want things in order feel threatened by anyone who leaves the smallest object out of place, and they become upset by any slightest disorder. Others become stifled when their lives become highly organized and regulated. They cringe at seeing anything that is out of place.

Others feel attacked by anyone who insists on perfect tidiness.

Everyone has a past. We need to perceive our present reactions, tensions, and emotions to see those roots from something from your past. Joy comes as we surrender it. That is how we turn weaknesses into opportunities. We can never manufacture joy. Joy is a by-product of relationships. It is quite possible to create an environment that allows joy to flourish. The movie and novel *Chocolat* have given me and the people who have used it in vision quests with me received clues on how to do just that.

Women glow when experiencing joy. We need to mix in that light. Joy and pleasure are essential to bring the magic of chemistry. Our connection will be more fun as we relate in joy. Masculine energy creates the most chemistry with an equal and opposite layer of feminine energy.

One of my female pastor friends informed me, "I am changing, but I'm not sure into whom or what or how." Her honesty and vulnerability surprised me. Change can be a challenge for women as well as men. This pastor said that she had experienced transformation as a liberation and a joy-filled experience.

Our culture sees change depicted as a struggle, inner turmoil, and an unhappy time. Our generation wants to just live through it. We look to arrive, not to journey toward an unknown destination.

Human friendship is the instrument for discipleship. We all yearn to be known. We want at last one person to grasp who we are. Healing the soul is made more difficult because that is our expectation.

Other people have power to deprive us of many things. We cannot blame others for what has not worked out. We must not reproach those in our relationship encounters for what we think they are depriving us of. We can strive to acquire spiritual autonomy by deepening our relationship with God. In these years of feminine and men's movement in various crises, life is not going well all around us, in the family, in the community, and in the church circle. We become discouraged and desire to give up. The power brokers can deprive us of using our gifts. This world's walls could collapse around us, but they could not rob us of praying, studying the Bible, and placing all our trust in God.

When I was working at the Sunday School Board, I was asked to review and promote a new book by W.A. Criswell, pastor of the First Baptist Church in Dallas, Texas. His book was titled, *Why I Preach That the Bible Is literally True*.
In each class at Vanderbilt, we were continually told that taking the Bible to be literally true was quite dangerous.

From childhood, I have respected the Bible. I firmly believe the text of the Bible is inspired. The Bible is there for every generation. The Bible as written for every language, every nation and territory, and every human being on earth. The text holds the mystery of salvation, of conversion, and of the kingdom of God in all its meaning, structure, and words. I had the joy of learning to read the Bible in its original Hebrew and Greek languages. I approach the Bible with utmost reverence.

Not only is the text of the Bible inspired, but the whole context is also inspired. The presence of God's Holy Spirit suffuses the text and let's the text enter our souls.

The Bible was written for conversion. The Bible was not written to inform but to convert. This biblical conversion is directed to the individual first and foremost. This is meant to be experienced within the context of community and he church. Conversion is about change. It brings healing to our souls. Understanding, knowledge, and insight is involved. To hear the Word of God is to change. If there is no changing, there was no hearing. If we keep sinning, we keep missing the mark.

The Spirit of Joy Church is a community of believers rededicating ourselves to bring in the kingdom of God. Reading the Bible is revolutionary. The God of scripture uses the works in God' work. The Good News comes to us, and God saves us. We then walk each other home to God.

The Bible should not be used to prove anything.

The gospels were written and disseminated as faith statements for already believing individuals. The Bible reminded the early Christians of what was the possibilities, the depth and meaning of their lives. The New Testament was written years after Jesus died. The gospels were intended for ordinary believers who found themselves in historical situations of persecution, of moral choices, and crises.

The resurrection of Jesus made eternal joy possible. That event provoked not only faith, but the hope and the love of the community, which was apparent among them. Together they were walking the walk and talking the talk and writing the words of life. The Bible is true because it calls us home.

Those who use the Bible to prove they interpret it correctly with cultural approval mix and match the words with their own selfish agenda. These people miss the spirit and common sense that the living Word explains. The Bible is not only about people who lived back then, but for people living now.

Transformation of the human soul involves the possibility that you might be wrong. When we share our interpretation of God's Word, we are aware that the spirit gave us the ability to discern the meanings. When we share, when we preach and teach others, we empty a sacred place inside our inner being and make room for the word of another in the free power of the Spirit, to enter and call us to conversion.

Contained within the biblical text is the truth about us and the undoing what we have become and for making something new of our lives. The Bible is the inspiring truth from the hand of humankind under the guidance of the Spirit of God. The Bible gives a record or handbook for becoming, unfinished and waiting to be grasped by the Spirit of God within our soul and in the souls of the community of believers Conversion and transformation make us more in the image of God.

There can be no real joy without the true understanding and acceptance of loss. Humans must lose or surrender in order to win. Get outside your comfort zone. Multicultural ministry looks for opportunities to be a minority. That's flames my own passion to travel. That's the only way to understand culture. I have learned more about other cultures just by doing life with people who differ from me.

Joy in Crossing Cultures

In cross cultural interaction, not only is it important for you to learn about other people, but it is also necessary that we know ourselves. We bring many assumptions into our conversations. Coming to understand our assumptions will help us to dump them.

Facial expressions do not mean the same thing in every nation. Modest dress in one culture is immodest dress in another culture. Women will profit from not wearing provocative clothing that exhibits their body emphasizing the lure of boobs and shapely legs. Colors have differing connotations. Touching one another is not the same everywhere.

The context you are living in today does not contain enough paths to accommodate the diversity. Your given pathways cannot reflect the breadth of what God is doing in your place.

God gives us the vision to change.

It changes our communication style. Change your current structures. Change who serves as a deacon, an elder, or the church board. Visioning takes patience. If we are not patient and careful, we can attempt to bring in sweeping changes without giving all the other people involved an opportunity to consider, process and prepare for changes.

Some cultures and churches love new things, and they react spontaneously. "We have always done it this way" is a common phrase, but it is never part of a joy vision quest for passionate seeking souls.

Before we present our vision, we need to know the congregation. We can observe how they respond to certain things. Learn how they have been doing things for a hundred years. Pay attention to what offends them. These relationships are important.

Reform, transformation, conversion, renewal, and change are beautiful when they lead to collaboration and joy.

We experience God doing new things in new ways, and we must respond in new ways. As times get rough, and they will, you will wonder if you are doing the right thing. If a church wants sameness, why not just let them stay the same.

Ministers of joy must become trailblazers. We must cut through the underbrush with a spiritual machete. Crazy feisty courage steps from the pastor to create something new. One of the most creative courses in preaching at Vanderbilt Divinity School was titled "Experimental Preaching." Those magnificent sermons preached in the classroom would not be welcomed in most congregations. Other congregations would enjoy them and stretch their faith.

Joy occurs as people go beyond their past approaches to see what God is doing. I enjoy hearing about the successes of many Vanderbilt graduates who have been used to change the church and the world.

Just because people discover the awareness of needed changes and they understand why change must happen, it does not mean they are ready.

It is quite possible at there are existing structures that have been in place for years that ae hurting your efforts. If you read the church bulletin for this next Sunday in many churches, everything will be exactly a duplicate of one created seventy years ago. That church and its members were there before you came, and they'll be there long after you leave.

When we feel discouraged, we remind ourselves that your church ministry was not your idea to begin with. The Word of God revealed this transforming idea. You are not responsible for crating unity. God has already accomplished that. Exhaustion comes as we cast a vision and try to explain why you are doing it. My own loved ones have said discouraging things about my ministry throughout the years. Some naïve folks even said, "Jim, you do not need to go to college to serve as a pastor. You sure don't need to know nothing to be a minister."

As you embrace my theological and practical concepts, ask God to give you the right perspective within each season. Nothing comes as a surprise to God. Remember you are not alone. There are people all around the world who are now pursuing the same vision as you are on a quest for joy. God will lead us through the valley to the place where you belong. Remember and be confident that the ways of God can be trusted. Keep on moving. Be courageous. Be strong. God will be there with us wherever we roam.

Relationships are important from our birth until our death. Encourage someone who needs what you still must give. Do not let the latter days of your life to be only about yourself. Ask God to guide you to somebody who needs hope. Give them your own hope. Inject joy into the pains of others. Writes emails, notes, and personal letter to the younger generation. Help every person you encounter to know that each one matters.

Men can experience joy in life now and eternally. Let us consider how joy is enhanced in the male. We have been living in a masculine crisis. It is also a feminine crisis. God's soul joins with our souls for creating and preparing people who believe for an eternity filled not with impossible problems, but an eternal joy.

Chapter Five

Enhancing Joy for the Masculine Soul

Let your life experiences penetrate you. Men who are wrapped up in their own thoughts, their own concerns miss the flow of life around them. Read II John 4. The writer was involved with his surroundings to notice and find joy in the lady's children. Listen and watch what is going on around you. Grace lifts. Grace brings joy. And what as we age, do we cherish more than joy? Men can experience rich thick joy in the simplest things.

Grandpas and grandmas see only the good qualities in their grandchildren. My grands always made me feel like there was no one she admired more. She heard me preach at Woodlawn Baptist Church when I was a young boy preacher. She noted that she just knew that I would be another Billy Graham.

Grandma Betty McReynolds hung on my words during my pre-teen years, when my words were halting and unsure. I adored her and recalled her gooseberry pies and Southern sweet ice tea.

Satchel Paige was a pitcher for the Kansas City Monarchs and later the Cleveland Indians. He was a man of joy. When he was called to play for Cleveland, nobody knew how old he was. Paige said, "Age is mind over matter. If you don't mind, it does not matter." We could write a book with these Paige sayings. Of a man's life he described as spills, drills, thrills, bills, ills, pills, and wills.

This colorful view really will not enhance joy for any man. Of course, every man's life differs as men grab onto each moment that brings joy. Men face differing experiences. That is what makes each man uniquely who he is. Each experience a man's experience to become stronger and ready for the next thing that comes along. Each unique encounter gives more strength and wisdom.

In the words of the Old Testament, people rejoiced at the birth of children. Read I Samuel 2. They found joy in friends. I Samuel 19:1. The knew joy in a faithful spouse. Proverbs 5:18. John the Baptist rejoiced in Jesus. John 17:13. Paul reminded the early Christians that they were his joy. Philippians 4:1

Enhance joy by writing down each of your joy experiences. The memories of joyful experiences renew the joy of the past as well as the present remain inside us and enrich us. Men are surprised by enhancing joy by strengthening communication with themselves, friends, and life partners. Men are required to constituently challenge outdated behaviors including fear, anger, and hate.

Joy is not attainable for stoic men. Men have the power to make changes. These days are tough and frustrating for men. The power resides inside. Happy men realize they are progressing. Write in a journal ten things that have the potential for joy. We males are the ones who take the leftovers home with us. However strange the masculine soul is viewed in our walled-up world, how much more are we to risk being a male. Do the required work as we gather and scatter that the ways we may go are the paths of God.

Joy never comes to those who despise themselves, but to those who affirm the person created by God. Humility is not self-denigration. Affirm yourself as you gain understanding. Pursue things that enhance your joy.

Transformation for men most often means surrendering the Fame. Power. Lust. Money. Pleasure. These things will not enhance a man's joy.

Enhancing the masculine soul involves going from our dream-sleep to an awakening. Man's ordinary state of consciousness is like a dreaming sleep compared to the awakened consciousness that is made possible. Poetic expressions include such words as "Our birth is but a sleep and a forgetting," by Wordsworth. Shakespeare wrote, "We are such stuff as dreams are made of."

While my wife and I were traveling through fairytale land in Germany, we stayed at Sleeping Beauty's castle. There really is a place in the Black Forest where we stayed and ate. The Grim brothers were said to have shared their fairy tales in that castle. "Sleeping Beauty" is a symbolic expression of his ancient teaching.

A man's soul has no awareness of mental processes. The soul simply flows along with the lines of habitual conditioning. Grim wrote, "If the eye never falls asleep, all dreams cease." The English poet William Blake gave us this insight: "If the doors of perception were cleansed, everything will appear to men as it is."

One of my fellow psychology students at the University of Oxford wrote, "All objects are seen and sensed to exist with a continuous, shimmering, dancing field of energy in motion, infinite and omnipresent."

Paul wrote that we see through a glass darkly, but then face to face. The apostle was writing of complete transformation of consciousness when self-perception is altered from self-images to self-realization.

The Christian symbol of the halo represents the energy phenomenon. Fear, anger, anxiety, and guilt have the effect of fixating the fluid processes of awareness in repeating routines.

Risk-taking Enhances Joy

There are risks in any potentially joy experience. We are mirror images of one another and our Creator. We see in others what we see in ourselves. One insight into who we are comes as we are aware of our friends. We are attracted by people who support us and reject those who do not. When we change our perception of the world, people react differently to us.

Meeting women can be a source for anxiety. Our worry leads to much discouragement. Men find joy in meeting and relating to an amazing female. We were strangers when we met and now there is something more to enhance joy. Gratitude is another source. Being thankful for all the good things in my life. Joy flows into our masculine souls. Joy brings men into the present moment.

Sharing joy with other people multiplies our own. Men light flames of joy when surrounded by joyful people. Men must be content with what they have. Just by living in the United States, men already have much more than most of the population of the world.

Music is a gateway as men let their music flow and allow it to express your own male self. Men are now asking; how can we sing the songs of life? Men enjoy singing with music on the radio. Sonia Sotomayor related the soul of music to our relationships with our children. "You really do need a parent who is willing to set themselves aside, and their own hopes and dreams. If your child marches to a different beat, a different drummer, you might just have to go along with that music. Help them achieve what's important to them."

Remember that work prepares a means to an end. Joy comes from friends, family, and the passion in our souls.

Changing my viewpoints of the world was an enormous risk. During times of turbulence in culture, politics, and religion, it is tempting to some to hold to their current convictions. The most difficult work involved is allowing change. (Rita Brock, "An Epidemic of Moral Injury," *The Christian Century*, September 8, 2021, pp. 26-30)

The quality of our risks depends on the amount of our fear. Outside events give us the opportunity to react. Most choose the fear. We give our fears power over us. We fear that problems can never be solved. We fear losing relationships. Our ego informs us that a lousy relationship is better than none. We run back to the comfort zones and our inaction empowers the fear. Nothing happens to correct the problem. Fear is the emotion that resists dealing with the moment. Risk is a component of growth and without it, we die inside. Once willing and able to risk, the rewards are worth it.

Risk is looking at a situation that appears hopeless and finding a way to make it work. Lessons are learned and new ways are accepted. Commitment to do something is positive risk. My own overriding fear has been rejection. The reason behind this is that we do not believe that we are strong enough or good enough to survive by ourselves.

We need to relate to others because we cannot do kingdom work by ourselves. We become isolated. The role of the church is a collusion. Men have now sold out to institutional preservation. We avoid issues which divide us. Men have been privatizing faith for generations. That selfish way causes men to perceive themselves as incapable and irresponsible. We need to become organized.

Isolated men lack nourishment. We complain and blame other people. We are trapped by self-preoccupation and complaining. If men want change, we must discover Jesus. Men must meet to discuss what love means and how it relates to all of us. The vision of the Spirit of Joy Church is to promote this process because it is the core of the Good News. Christ's church ought and sometimes is, the place where connection and exploration happen.

Joy is enhanced as souls go from fragmentation to wholeness. Finding wholeness in a fragmented world is the vision statement for the Christian Church (Disciples of Christ) in the United States and Canada. Our human condition in this rapidly changing world is described as scattered, dispersed, and torn. Wholeness brings the soul from separation to oneness. The Gospel of Thomas, which was left out of the biblical canon, declared: "When you make the male and female into a single one, so that the male will not be male, and the female not be female, then shall you enter the kingdom of God." (Ronald Roberts, "Metaphors for the Transformation of Human Consciousness," *The Journal of Transpersonal Psychology*, pp. 54-56)

For men joy enhances the transitional crises. Crisis is a signal for despair and discouragement or challenges to change. Instead of seeing the times of challenge as when things are going wrong, we can view these times as periods in our lives when things can finally go right. Crises are tamed by masculine conversion that brings healthy readjustment.

As men we need joy. There are no beginnings without endings. No love without loneliness. No health without illness. The world comes to be what we have imagined.

Without demonizing others, we can find healing that matters. The mystery means males as well as females must take God seriously. There exists an impulse within every man to repair relationships. Men "need" to do just that. The Spirit has made us aware of the connection. Men have the compassion to pick up the victims. Some men let the thick walls in this world interfere with that impulse, but it is woven into the masculine soul. God can produce music out of anything or even out of nothing.

"I think I should have no other mortal wants, if I could always have plenty of music. Music seems to infuse strength into my limbs, and ideas into my brain. Life seems to go on without effort, when I am filled with music," classical writer George Eliot said.

The improvising creativity of God merges with our limited creativity. Men discover ways to do something different. In that our work and our humble little ministries express a connection with God.

In the process of transformation or conversion, men must wrestle with that inner temptation that causes us to take God less seriously than we take ourselves and God's image that is also within us. Martin Buber called this phenomenon "the evil urge." So, this issue that is real in every man, including in Jesus who was temped as we are. Evil is not irreversible. Overcoming evil is what salvation is about.

There is huge difference between talking and reconciliation. Serious and open dialogue may not be successful, but it certainly improves the odds. Men need courage to remain in the discussion. Men become cowards as they keep setting on the sidelines because this crisis is terribly difficult. Men conclude that reconciliation is impossible. Julie Harris said, "God comes to us in the way we communicate with each other, whether it be a symphony orchestra, or a wonderful ballet, or a beautiful painting, or a play. It is a way to express our humanity."

The insights of feminist thinkers are provocative. Creating beauty is a dimension of creativity. This is evident in music, literature, and the arts. Living in the strength of the joy of God is existing with creativity. That is experiencing God. Feminist theologians affirm that. A clergywoman suggested, "Great poets need a great audience." A poem needs to connect. This book needs to connect. Without your support, my creativity has been in vain.

Chapter Six

Loving the Gift of a Man's Daughter or Son

The relationship between father and daughter is nurtured with love. My hearts melted when I first held my daughter. When my wife told me she was pregnant, I became overjoyed. Somehow God told me my child would be a girl.

I was smitten instantly. During my lifetime, Linda and I have shared special times. We have had daddy-daughter dates. We have traveled together. We studied the globe of the earth together. We have explored new things and places including church buildings and basilicas where we roamed around to take in all we could. Sometimes we would sit on the floor viewing family photos. I enjoyed reading to her, teaching her how to write and to discover her own gifts. Some things, such as teaching her to ride her bike, resulting in Linda's saying one day as she rode her bike, saying, "I taught myself." I still have her artwork, keepsakes, and cards and notes we have written to each other. A cherished ritual was for me to give her a good-bye kiss every morning before my day began. One day when she was small, somehow, I left the house without the kiss. Linda was so disappointed. Her mom called me at work to tell me how disappointed Linda was. On that cold winter day, I excused myself from work and walked back home in the snow to reassure her how much I loved her.

I am blessed that my Linda and I have an unconditional loving relationship. With all the broken relationships and family disruption, I am optimistic that joy will prevail in our constantly changing world. More fathers encourage daughters to reach their potential than in any other time.

There is not much written about the father-daughter relationship as there has been about fathers and sons.

Our relationship, like any other, was never perfect. I am sharing our record and strivings as a model for others. Perhaps my sharing our story, this book can be used by today's fathers with small daughters to have the joy and love from God to create surprising miracles. As I explore my life with Linda, other fathers and some mothers, can explore theirs as well.

We are like any other loving pair. We have tried to harmonize being right with each other. In God's guidance, the wounds will be allowed to heal rather than being kept open. Our goal and vision quest are to give each other valuable insights, then healthy fathers and daughters free each other to live healthy lives. The separate lives will share common ground. There will be disruptions and strains during transitional periods. Linda was never a rebellious teen. And neither was her son Ethan, who is now a college student. Even a near perfect parent-child relationship must be engaged in an imperfect world.

The day in August when I first held our bundle of joy, I bonded with her. We must have viewed each other as perfectly flawless beings. Mutual adoration remains for quite a long time. We both learn we are not perfect. We set limits. As part of the process, each of us accept, forgive, know, and rejoice that we are individuals and equals. Linda enjoyed participating as a Brownie scout and as a summer camper. When Linda was eight, her mom and I went for a vacation in Colorado without Linda. We had never not been "the three of us," bonded and proud to be a family.
Her mother never left home even to attend church for the first six months of Linda's life.

Every transcendence requires compassion, wisdom, forgiveness, and acceptance. The English poet Shelly rote, "Love makes all things equal." In terms of the joy they give each other, they do begin as equals. In my eyes, she was perfect. My soul united with the wonder of her existence to stir my impulses to feeling love like no other.

My infant daughter adored me as well. I remember the day Linda looked deep into my eyes as if looking into my soul saying quietly, "Daddy." She and I played pick-a-boo. She would enter our bedroom and say, "Linda has gone." She'd climb into the sheets and play like she had disappeared. I would pretend that I could not see her. We were quite happy. We kept smiling at each other. Linda only wanted my presence. Loving a daughter is to fully validate her by cheering her on as she learns to sit up, crawl, stand, walk, talk, and later other events like riding her bicycle or swimming. A child carries in her heart and soul the experience when she was first greeted.

The wonder of our days in the womb is a continuous miracle we are privy to in some ways. Nothing prepares us for the moment of arrival. Each one is unique, amazing, and special. The gestation time is a divine miracle. From conception to delivery, we live, move, and have our being in God as well as the watery home of our mother's womb.

Other people label us and set life norms for us based on our gender. Parents inadvertently model these norms. Some tell little girls to walk like a lady. We tell sons to never cry, don't throw the ball like a girl. A little boy's worst insult is to be called a girl.

I realized from the beginning that my relationship with Linda would involve changes. She would be a little less affectionate. She would be more interested in her friends and less entertain by me. She might even find me embarrassing. At one time, she did not want me to share anything about our life journey with others, not even in my books. Both of us now see my words to minister to new fathers and new mothers the roles they play, to give them love, nurture, and support they need. My daughter is irreplaceably important to me. It is a joy to be in her life.

In the *Ninja Warrior* competition that features unbelievable athletic performances, one man on the nationally televised show had seven daughters. Seven. No sons. This strong father had created a home filled with love. His seven daughters ran to him when he arrived from work each day. They jumped all over him to his delight.

I have taught her to learn from her experiences. I taught her when to be cautious. I have taught her that she is equal to her husband. I helped her take risks that builds her confidence. I have tried to remind her of what she does not remember. I taught her the importance of being a lady. She often told me that she wanted to always be lady-like. I have taught her that women and men can be good friends.

When a Daughter Establishes Her Own Home

Life is not the same when a daughter establishes her own home. They must plan to get together. Linda was born when I was 28 years old. Now she is a parent. She has journeyed from infancy to adult gone through education, initiated her career, her love life, and enough joys and sorrows to fill a dozen novels. There is much to share. Both come to know, forgive, and enjoy each other as separate persons.

One day Linda told me she had turned out right. Indeed. She was the valedictorian in her high school, Phi Beta Kappa in college, and a law school graduate and editor of the law review. She is an amazing mother, wife, and corporate lawyer in Washington, D.C. We now live separate but equal lives. We are intimate yet appropriately distanced.

She is precious, unique, loving woman, and the world needs her. There is not enough darkness in this world to snuff out the joyous light of one candle. Her feminine and masculine energies are in balance. This has been demonstrating in all the stages and experiences of her life.

When I die, Linda may feel abandoned but simultaneously set free. By now, we have both lost parents. With our faith in God, our relationships have been loving. Preparation for the joy has gone on from the start. Linda has always been a free spirit. She joyed in being allowed to play in the lawn with nobody to watch. She felt safe in crossing the street without her hand being held. She walked with other children by herself to kindergarten. Each separation was a foreshadow of the final one on earth.

Saint Joseph: A Model for Men

Saint Joseph, the father of Jesus, gave us guidance. Joseph paints a vivid portrait that helps us fathers understand, appreciate, and grow closer to the man who enabled your birth. The Bible has no spoken words of Joseph. Each gospel mentions him. We learn about Joseph as we reflect on his child Jesus. Could we say stepchild?

For most of Jesus' life he lived in a home that Joseph the carpenter probably built.
That home is the place Jesus prayed, lived, ate, celebrated, and shared with his brothers and sisters. Just as my daughter's words and deeds reflect my guidance and love for her, Joseph was known through Jesus' words and deeds.

Joseph risked everything to care for Jesus and Mary. Read Ephesians 5:25-30.

Joseph was a man who saw in all members of Christ's body the child he helped raise. This masculine soul must not be forgotten.

Joseph gave new meaning to what a father is to be. Jesus in turn would show us what God the Father is. Joseph is the masculine soul whom God calls to participate in the plan of salvation. Joseph was touched by an angel. He was awakened with his inner hunger for eternal life. His visit with the angel emphasizes for us the way God always takes the first step. Every father and mother long for the eternal. Only God can answer to that longing.

God gives a sense of hope beyond positive thinking or human sentiment. Joseph's human fatherhood reflects what living in God's purpose means. This man lives the tension between the salvation that Jesus represents and the experiences of present world conditions and circumstances.

Every daughter and son arouse the thought of what might be. That thought moves us beyond our limitations and experiences. The smile of a child goes beyond the walls of uncertainty and fear. Fathers and mothers will pass from habituating in this world. Joseph died knowing God trough his son Jesus. My dear departed brother David's theme in life was "love is forever." Joseph dedicated his life to "the love that never ends." The never-ending love of God poured into his heart in tangible ways. In Joseph's modest home, Jesus developed "in wisdom and in stature, and in favor with God and man."

Lowliness of heart helped Joseph live without concern for the future nor the past.

Joseph lived in this peace that goes beyond human understanding in the most trying circumstances. He had an inner awareness because the Spirit of God lived in his soul.

Mothers and father in our rapidly changing world must follow Joseph's example in walking each other to their eternal home.

Jesus was born into a simple home. Joseph nor most of us are in no way destitute, but we are not in the one per cent in our possessions or power. My wife and I searched for a home in Saint Joseph, Missouri. The one we finally bought was on a street called Linda Lane.

Within the walls of the world there exist radical conditions of poverty, which brings on helplessness that can not break down the walls of the world. God entrusted Joseph with the health and well-being of Jesus.

The mystery and transcendence are obfuscated by our radical preoccupation with the fulfillment of our desires. Most men and women see only themselves. In terms of our modern social media, we are required to insist and strive for respect and restraint.

Joseph was a pure-hearted man because he accepted the will of God. This father, like faithful fathers in our time, beheld the face of God every day. While I was a student at Carson-Newman University, I served as a student minister of prayer working with Dr. Charles Trentham at the First Baptist Church in Knoxville, Tennessee. He often advised that manual labor is good for the soul." I labored each day in labor at the Carson-Newman cafeteria. When I look back, this part of my schooling is one of the most joyful parts in my preparation for my ministry and my life. Jesus was given a suitable home. Imagine Jesus' recall of his work with Joseph as the insight for his words about building on a foundation in one of his parables.

Joseph, Mary and all Jesus' brothers and sisters' lives required careful attention. Read Luke 14:28, 33. Jesus knew the world's condition. Nazareth did not protect him from fallen humanity. It did provide him material for his stories.

Imagine being the father that taught Jesus how to use a hammer. Joseph must have watched anxiously the first time Jesus used a saw. The Roman Empire controlled most of the known world in Jesus' time. Joseph had to walk a narrow line to follow what he believed and lived rather than those held in the empire world.

Where two or three are gathered together, or as we now say, "when two or 20 gather," you will find differing thoughts about being in community, the theology of salvation, or finding the way to be one body. Churches and spiritual groups have experienced splits, reforming, creeds, disputations, schisms, and corruption.

I have preached to only two people about 20 times in my long years of preaching.
At least one other person is required to call our message a sermon. After my retirement, I continue to worship with a small group that we call the Spirit of Joy Church. I support both male and female pastors with the opportunities they and I are given. That is the reason I continue to write books such as this one.

My daughter, my wife, my clergywomen friends have taught me that the way men and women give up their power is by thinking that they have no power. Barbara Bush, mother and wife of two United States presidents said, "At the end of your life you will never regret not having passed one more test, winning one more verdict, or not closing on one more deal. You will regret time not spent with a husband, a child, a friend, or a parent." Barbara Bush has spoken to women within the richness of human experience.

The feminine soul moves through time and space. Women have revealed to me some of the sagas of profound joys and the struggles experienced during their lifetimes. Those joys and loves prepare us for eternity. "Love is a flower that grows in any soil, works its sweet miracles undaunted by autumn frost or winter snow, blooming fair and fragrant all the year, and blessing those who give and those who receive," observed Louisa May Alcott. I enjoy the words of Zora Neale Hurston, "Love makes your soul crawl out from its hiding place."

Love must be our foundation if we are to solve the problems we are now facing. If we do not love each other by giving and taking without restrictions, our ministries are not actions of love, but an unhelpful transaction. Alice Walker said, "It is so clear that you have to cherish everyone. I think that is what I get from these black women, that every soul is to be cherished, that every flower is to bloom."

Men and women together have the right to love and be loved. Willa Cather, our famous writer from Nebraska wrote, "Only solitary men know the full joys of friendship. Others have their family; but to a solitary and an exile his friends are everything."

In books I have been transformed to other worlds and other eras. Books help us to understand and live in our own worlds. My daughter and I both love books. I read as many as I could during her childhood. We continue to give each other gifts of books.

Why a Daughter Needs a Dad

One of my most treasured books from my daughter is the one titled *Why a Daughter Needs a Dad*. I have quoted from it often in sermons, seminars, and some of my books. Linda is my inspiration for what I do right and not wrongs.

The photographs are well worth the price of the book. They were taken by Janet Lankford-Moran from Nashville, Tennessee. Some of the best words are a daughter needs her dad "so she learns that men are trustworthy, to teach her that men and women can be good friends, to teach her the joy of serving others, to teach her the importance of being a lady, to remind her of the comfort of being held near and feeling secure, to remind her of what she may not remember, to be the history of her family for her own children, to let her know that while she might not be the center of someone else's world, she is the center of his."

I have pondered the deep inspiration for being a dad and a man by Gregory Lang. Let me share a few more. "A daughter needs a dad to prepare her to persevere through hardship, to help her take the risks that will build her confidence, to protect her when she is not wise enough to protect herself, to tuck her in at night, to show her she will have at least one hero who will not let her down, to teach her she is equal to her husband, to influence her life even when he isn't with her, to show her how it feels to be loved unselfishly, to tell her truthfully that she is the most beautiful of all, to teach her to accept e differences in others, to teach her to weigh the consequences of her actions and make decisions accordingly, to make the family whole and complete, to never think she is too old to need him, to teach he that her value as a person is more than he way she looks, to learn that when he says it will be okay soon, it will." (Gregory E. Lang, *Why a Daughter Needs a Dad,* pages not numbered)

The most miraculous gifts are our daughters and sons. Without them, we would laugh less. We would not have innocence. We would hold less hope. We would shrivel and vanish. I see my daughter on every page. This work, including the awesome pictures, has inspired me to embrace the challenging role that men have to give women nurture, love, and support.

These are gifts of love. They are reciprocated time after time. Men who have daughters—or sons—will always have the pleasure of being in their lives. Perhaps there is a talented woman who could write the same inspiration for the sons in their lives.

Chapter Seven

Walking Each Other Home

In the past decades theology has changed. Some of our theological understandings have changed. One Hebrew professor at Vanderbilt said when I was studying at Vanderbilt Divinity School told us in a group that he didn't know what theology meant. Theologians today are still examining traditional texts and beliefs to include women whenever possible. We have experienced many changes with the Vatican Council, the feminist movement, and the liturgical and theological language to be inclusive and descriptive of gender reality. Feminist theology has taught that women are to be remembered and imitated, not because they are somebody's mother or wife, wife, or daughter, but on their terms of identification. At the height of the energetic feminist movement, women could almost fill their seminary degree requirements by taking course in feminism, womanist theology, history of women in preaching and topics that affirmed women as leaders.

Perhaps our racial, gender, and theological divisions are showing more than we perceive in current theologizing. Our faith is now reaching the lost, the uncounted, the forgotten. The study of theology is an act of justice and courage. Self-worth and renewed confidence are tools for every person's voice. The Spirit shows us hat the way of God does not include easy solutions or magic moments or even immediate change. Radical changes do take time even with the rapidly changes happening now.

Feminist Theology and the Realities of Life.

Feminist theology arises out of life's realities. This theology goes beyond suppression. Still, it is expressed with feminine tenderness. The feminist theologian opens herself to full communion. She offers compassion. Feminist theology calls for powerful passion.

Walking and gathering with each other, people do not believe oppression is the primary problem. The crisis is much more complicated. Women who see gender as the focus of oppression begins with certain assumptions that most women refuse to accept. Most refuse domination by anybody, male or female. The problem of domination includes sexism, materialism, individualism, racism, politics, and economics.

Our ethics and practices must be examined through the lens of serving not getting.

We need to walk together to build community support and justice. Our theology and our spirituality requires the Holy Spirit that blows where spirit wills, not in the homes among those already in dominance now. The theology that makes us more human and divine, most aware of and caring for others, most caring and listened to truly is the correct one.

Men and women ponder in their souls what the tenderness of God is. That would be the most effective theology that works for us all.

Women and men alike have the same goal. Our souls will not be satisfied until we know the "joy of the Lord" brings the possibility of heaven-like happiness and joy now in the ever-changing world. We feel stuck in the loop of our minds to figure out how to solve problems. The mind alone or strategies will not replace the power inside of us with energy and intelligence. We refuse to act on our inner knowing. My wife, my daughter, and my supportive friends helped me develop a bond with my inner compass. Loving communion remains the hallmark of living.

The walls in this world will not tumble down. Men must embrace vulnerability, create strong relationships, and live joy-filled lives. The masculine in both women and men walk through the world to discover themselves and to figure out the knowledge, wisdom, acceptance, grace, love, passion, and joy. Just because we have missed the mark ever since the Fall does not excuse us from trying to redeem, convert, and transform the world.

Influencing the World of the Future.

There is an energy building that involves changing roles, to be willing to play the part of influencing the world of the future. We work together to actualize the possibilities that lie within us. Traditional roles of women and men have changed.
Every human is now being freed up. Dormant energy has been ignited. Walking each other home in the unhappy are being collectively united. Whispers inside us are being realized that can heal every soul. We must respond to these yearnings. God the Creator and every diverse human being have the same goals and intentions.

Journeying through the new world order has no realistic map. We must create a model together. Our current world is not aware of the new landscape or any options to the way humans live. I am seeking to enable my grandson, my daughter, and those I love to be whatever they want to be. Both women and men sense the same things. We hear the spiritual yearnings of our souls, but we don't know what to do. When we unlock the source of power that we have never enjoyed before in history.

Begin your spiritual journey anew each day. I can't emphasize enough how much we must leave the past with out weaknesses, failures, sins. If a person falls a hundred times a day, begin again with new awareness of what needs to be done. Think about that.

In times of discouragement, we feel we have failed again and again. Nothing you have ever done, nowhere you have ever been, can ever stop you from turning in the healing direction. One of the women who ran in a challenging race around Elmwood made a wise statement. She said that if one looks back, she cannot run. Runners, just try to run while you look back over your shoulder. You will give up. Try it. I did and I fell over.

Discouragement is a danger in these changing times. Do not strive for an impossible perfection. Focus on what is now at hand. Show yourself joyful even when you have physical problems. Physical pain diverts our attention.

Reaction and response at times of discouragement or dissatisfaction may cause us to overreact or ignore it. Focus on how far you have come and the joy of the journey, not on how far you have left to go. We must all develop our discernment muscle. Separate the wheat from the chaff, truth from spin, substance from fluff.

Both Sexes Share the Same Issues

Every created human is restless to attract intimate relationships with God and others where we can develop our authentic real selves. I taught my daughter that she could become whatever she wanted. She developed herself day by day, stage by stage, to find her anointed place in this walled up world. She struggled to let herself be supported in her search for happiness. She felt a burning flame to express her gifts and graces to make a difference in the world. Linda had supportive friends in her chosen world. Some of our daughters feel walls in their worlds as barriers they cannot work through. Linda has always wanted to help the world become a better place.

Our current emotional reactions and feelings of restlessness and misery are symptoms of the awakenings to new stages. We can pursue our own destiny. The walls of the world have held back women, people of color, the elderly, and the disabled for eons.

Adults find gender is constraining. A woman might be complimented for what she is wearing. Men usually are complimented for their helpful ideas. We have discovered a deep disconnection from themselves. Adults chafe at assumptions. We cite a woman's beauty and a man's character. These are unfortunate assumptions that reflect sexism.

We all need to discuss more using ourselves to express how we think and feel about issues and the possibilities of who we are. We deeply desire to share our talents with others. Happiness in life requires us to belong, to express ourselves, to be alive, to contribute. Women, and now men as well, struggle for becoming equals. The world needs both sexes to give fulfillment to both men and women. United together to attain the same goals, we have the power to shape the future.

Women are transformed to discover unique things inside themselves. They are seeing joyous things through the eyes of others. Now I fully know that others matter. Being equals gives women their own authentic voices as they know connection and not separation, understanding and acceptance beyond assessment.(Mary Field Belenky, *Women's Ways of Knowing; The Development of Self, Voice, and Mind,* p. 229)

Women who find new methods of foreseeing for themselves "a room of their own," as Virginia Woolf called this transformation. Women create life worth living in family, community, church, work, and the world. Strong women aspire to working to contribute to the empowerment and improvement of the lives of others. They now feel a part of the effort to address with others the burning issues of the day.

If we use the same methods, we will just become further frustrated. Together we can discover who we are, our purpose, our spirituality connections, our flourishing, our relationships will mirror our values. We need to connect to our feminine and masculine powers to tear down the walls we have constructed in our world.

We must continue to share our inner wisdom. Together we will gain the courage and confidence to take risks and to become our potential in our clearest moments.
Our walls of barriers are not outside of us. We blame changing society and circumstances for our failures. We have been designing forms of blame.

It is a waste of time trying to fit where we fit in in today's world. We ere wonderfully and fearfully and uniquely created. The world's walls insist on passive behavior. We can live with active, exciting behavior. This is transformation, conversion, and self-realization. We are not hopeless or helpless. There is a tomorrow. Our mistakes do not cause us to be useless for the rest of our lives. I have not always able to "count it all joy." Dead ends are preludes to new beginnings. Knowing this truth is both the fulfillment of our life journeys and the doorway to still greater expansion.

Being young. Staying young. Feeling young. I enjoy being with female ministers who are in their twenties. Soon these lovely souls continue to bring freshness to lives. By the forties, there comes gray hairs, aching joints, and new pain. In the fifties, you begin to sense the inevitable. By the sixties, we are fully aware tat our life is soon to be over. In the seventies and eighties, we are well-seasoned versions. What does it take to stay young while years quickly move toward our final time?

Cultivate beauty and joy now whatever your present age. Listen to beautiful music.

Music keeps our souls young. Filling our souls with music embraces the eternal essence of all that is fresh, new, and alive. Walk and talk with others. If we are breathing, there is something new to learn. Listen to the opinions of others who are in every age. Keep traveling to places where you have never been.

Life responds to us.

Our life journey is not happening to us. Life responds to us. Love will not come if we think we are unlovable. My wife has taught me so many things. She has a powerful intuition. Most women and men are disconnected from our intuition. Even when we sense an inner knowing, we lack the flashes to distinguish between where our inner thoughts are coming from either inner wisdom or from our fear.

So often we hear in this ever-changing world that our faith and tradition is void of strong female examples and heroes. Try to read only about feminine warriors in the Bible as luminaries to help guide women and men in our unique paths to eternity.

The women God called to bring the chosen people into the world were ordinary women who struggled with oppression, infertility, emptiness and loss, yet found the hope and strength in the joy of the Lord to share they did. We must see what we can learn from the witness of women who went before us to pass on the faith.

Women express the joy of our salvation. They are true women of the Word. Read Psalm 1 and Jeremiah 17. Women knew and followed the Word of God. Women are strong trees planted by streams of water, which withstand times of drought.

Their courage bears spiritual fruit. That fruit is shared on our earth journey. I am grateful for the women who have mothered me. Women have stepped into the gap when men failed them. Women brought beauty from ashes.

The more things change, the more they stay the same. Situations that women have found themselves in are worlds away from what we are experiencing today. Human nature is the same. We face similar dilemmas and temptations that have existed in all generations.

Women are now fueled with an inner fire, communicating to the world with exhilaration and optimism as they plunge ahead to a wholesome future.

It is now time for humankind to profit from the witness of women who have gone before us. It is now women's turn to shine. My grandson Ethan gave me a posture that hangs in the center of my office displays. It read: "Find joy in your journeys."

Women now enjoy a perspective of personal authority in a blend of their unique life circumstances and attributes. As a result the relationships and self-concepts have dramatically changed for both women and men.

Chapter Eight

THE AUTHOR'S PERSONAL TRANSFORMATION

My inner work to find my real self has been aided by spiritual directors, fellow men and women, psychological testing such as Myers-Briggs, MMPI, birth order, enneagram groups, and spirituality, prayer, worship, repentance, relationships, unique experiences, taking risks, achievements, education, and acceptance of who I am.

I am thankful to live in the wall of the world of hopes, feelings, and dreams. The intangibles are the most important. I now think in analogies and metaphors with vivid pictures from a whole perspective that allows me to continue to see a complete picture. I love to use my skills to create and explore possibilities.

I now ponder every alternative, brainstorming with others. I function from my right brain. I enjoy being different with my rare personality. My life is being converted by my vision. I am now trying to support my visions with facts. My intuition has served me well. I see more beauty and wonder and even purpose of my existence.

I have gained a desire to enable the world to be different and better. Quality of life for others—women, all races, opposing politics, and the rigid church—are more important today than before. I perceive my true self as warm, loved, gentle, and living with positive emotions. My intimate friendships remain deep and lasting. I try to find common ground with those who oppose or differ from me. I have been made so sensitive to others' feelings that they become my own. I remain vulnerable to the emotional manipulation of those who want to use or dominate me.

No person wants to face rejection. If I ask somebody to write a review of one of my books or to write a foreword or an afterword, I feel a twinge of rejection. Whatever two people can give each other is always enough. Over the long haul, rejection continues.

I have begun to cultivate a system of friends and support so have more than just one or two people to lean on. That's going easy on myself. Admit if the rejection hurt you. Everyone experiences rejection at one time or another. Seek the support you need, then move on.

Masculine Path to Joy

I have many memories of riding my red bike. The wind blew gently in my face. I never stressed over the height of the curb. I assumed that I could make it all the way to downtown Bristol and back. I felt strong in my legs. The possibility of a car or truck wiping me out never crossed my boyhood mind. I had one wreck. I had my brother on the back of my bike. I stirred around a sharp curve, and we fell over. My brother broke his arm. We took some time telling our mother. She had warned against us riding on the same bike.

I have been blessed by angels. I remember and attain many of my childlike qualities. Wonder. Innocence. Curiosity. Passion. Good times. Enjoying myself. Bringing a smile to others. Feeling a lightness of being. I remember my lasting joy as I preached my first sermon at age 12. I enjoyed my first published book at age 17.

I am fortunate to have so many experiences of joy. I was taught to have goals, to work hard, to achieve. My continuous path to joy left me memories. Now I am too old to do things I do not care to do. My well-worn joy path is not dependent on any accomplishment or life situation. Joy has become my way of being. Even if I wanted to, I cannot push boulders up a hill. Taking a stand for the joy God has given me still requires courage. My personal affirmation to live in happiness requires discipline and trust. Some experiences have needed transformation. I greet each day in expectation of joy. My vision has kept me on the joy path.

Life is our pilgrimage. Watching God at work never gets old. I have often needed to gain perspective on what was happening in my own life and where God was calling me next. I do my own vision quests as I travel with others in a powerful connection with God's people. God will fill us with courage for living the life we were born to live.

My journey captures the meaning of Paul's words to the Philippians 2:13, which I now translate into "For it is God who keeps on working in you." As my childhood pastor used to say, "Keep on keeping on." Read Psalm 13:1, 5-6.

I have never liked conflict. I have been transformed to accept the fact that some dislike me. As an introvert, I now accept my quiet, reserved, calm, and shy self. I am more careful with whom I share my deepest feelings. A harmonious environment is important to my flourishing. Life has been emotionally brutal to me. I know it is fine to withdraw into my own world just to survive.

Life without Love

Life without love is frightening. Rejection is devasting to me. I am being converted from self-condemnation. I fear that people will use my vulnerability against me. Forgiveness has lifted resentment from holding on to past hurts. I do less self-destructive behaviors that continues feeling of never being enough.

I wish you well on your journey toward transformation, self-understanding, healing, surprising joy, hope, and contentment. With humility, I have thought back and reflected on the choices I have made that changed the course of my life forever. The choices I have made has determined the quality of my life. There are no regrets. Each experience or situation has led me to cherish eternal life.

Every human being on earth needs to change thoughts, habits, and emotions that hold us back. Acceptance of who we are. Embracing the wisdom held inside. Learning to love the uniqueness with which we exist in the world. A destiny of aggression is not born. It is carefully taught and created and free to rein. The feminine parts of our souls can be the way to raise nonviolent boys.

Our spiritual journeys include the opportunity to discover the untapped riches that lie within every soul. I am grateful for enjoying a loving daughter, wife, and friends. Women have shared experiences about being hurt by aggressive men. My women friends have helped me to know that there is life after pain. They taught me to bring all my emotions to the surface. The feminine and the converted masculine turns pain and suffering into purpose if I make a conscious effort to do so.

I have used my gifts and graces to gain courage to write on topics that no one is talking about. The rigid ideas of religion and culture has been the source of teaching on femininity and masculinity. Love has been made impossible. Men and women do yearn to free themselves from the cultural cages.

We so want everything to be permanent. Ponce de Leon searched for a fountain of youth. That does not exist. We seek permanence in our jobs and in friendships. We seek permeance in attitudes, feelings, and belief systems. We want everything fixed for life.

There must be a balance between desiring life to be predictable and permanent and expect everything to change simultaneously. All relationships end. Life transitions come at least every ten years. Your best friend today may not be your best friend tomorrow. The company you work or the congregation you serve is not likely where you will be in less than five years. We will never find anyone who understands us. There is no going back into the womb.

My own transformation reveals my vulnerability, insight, and courage in dismantling the walls of stifling patriarchy. My now integrated soul gets louder to provide more freedom and love for myself among men. And among women.

Talking with women. Reading books by women. Praying for women in my life. I find so much hope and inspiration inevitably emerging. Women's struggles for equality. Quest for knowledge. Unconditional love for family. Balancing work and family. Value of optimism. Meaning of friendship. Exploring despite the risks and dangers.

We live in a rapidly changing world. We can change and grow and still be who we are. We learn how to adjust to the changes. We know we can face life with confidence, knowing we will have to surrender ourselves in the process.

I have managed to say goodbye to my past. I can say hello to today, my present, and experience the joy. Previous joy experiences induce pleasantness as we recapture the joys I have experienced. Joy has left a positive residue that enables me to think and feel better about my relationships.

I have been converted to draw emotional capital in all troubling times. I consciously remind myself of the joys. I suggest people play those video tapes that will be forever in our minds and to put the negative tapes on the shelf.

My life is not particularly difficult. It is not always exciting or filled with passion. I recognize that life has cycles of highs and lows. These cycles are now received gladly. Both joy and disappointment are essential in preparation for eternal life.

Joy energizes me. It is my motivation to redirect my life. With each bit of success in my calling from God, I get a renewed sense of joy. Joy times increase my capacity to relate warmly and intimately with others.

The heart that loves is always young. I have known people for a while, and I assume they were in their twenties, but later found they were forty. At times the opposite happened. I have thought a member of my congregation was in her late forties, but I was told they were in their early thirties. Perhaps I was reading their attitude. A joyful and loving attitude makes people seem younger than their years. A negative life attitude subtracts years from life.

Joy changes all of us. It makes us complete. "God isn't finished with me yet" is my message to those with whom I communicate. An experience of joy has revealed unknown aspects of me that has given me courage. I know the people who are attracted to me also hold on to a positive frame of mind. My relationships improve when my joy is shared. Even my relationships with strangers or those much different from me have improved.

In one of my mentor Dr. John Killinger's sermons, he talks about Brother Lawrence who composed *The Practice of the Presence of God.* Brother Lawrence gave the insight that his greater joy was to sense the presence of God. Joy and spirituality nurture each other.

Joy brings us closer to God. And the closer we get to God, the more joy we experience. Read Psalm 16:11.

The Wonder of Eternal Joy

Joy proves to us that joy is a here and now emotion. And each time I find myself in a joy, I ponder what eternal joy with God must be like.

My own journey continues as my experiences and interpretations are added to those of other seekers. My journey is like some Nebraska farmland that needs to be overturned, dug into, seeded, watered and tended with care.

This book reflects sharing stories, reading books, and practicing what was heard. We stand in the presence of God to be seen and counted, both as individuals and together, for what we are and what we are not yet. My positive thinking hero, Norman Vincent Peale, related, "One of the greatest moments in anybody's developing experience is when he no longer tries to hide from himself but determines to get acquainted with himself as he really is."

I find that my life improves with age. Jane Powell said, "I feel like an ostrich who has finally pulled its head out of the sand and loves what he sees I enjoy getting older, life gets easier every day."

Getting older means we get to do exactly what we want, when we desire to do it. A transformed life is positive delicious. Joy means growing older with grace. Nagarjuna said, "When young, rejoice in the tranquility of the old." One of the things I enjoy is a gathering of my retiree friends. Quite honestly, I get more zest for these older friends than anything else. I marvel at their acquired wisdom and rich experience.

The difference in my personal transformation and my continuous conversion is that I look for the ultimate joy not just a struggle. We can reimagine personal transformation to give us an eternal happiness. It has been heartwarming to encounter women who are in this time with me.

Together we have found a way to be faithful to God and our contemporary situation at the same time. My lady-like daughter, my wife, and my female friends turn my attention to the unnamed people, whose stories in the Bible are overlooked.

We have lived in an environment with a tendency to spiritualize, personalize, and theologize the biblical texts rather than share what they really say.

Preaching and teaching the Bible is about unity, balance, churches filled with the joy, harmony, peace, and wholeness. Faithful interpretations bring about forgiveness, restoration, reconciliation, justice, and mercy. The word conversion describes the stories we need to repeat, and when we need to let go and let our souls be reformed and refashioned.

I have been reconciled bringing me to a foundation of unity as my eyes focus on equality, care of the poor, and the honor of the Spirit of God. In every new generation, men and women are required to rethink and reevaluate our spiritual and theological sayings. The Word of God is a living, breathing, present reality that moves us to passionately follow Jesus and women such as Jessie in John's Killinger's excellent novel.

Together we shall discover the kingdom of God hidden between the walls of suffering and death within the world.

This is a part of ministry and life that all of us must accept and deal with consistently. We must stay clear in healthy ways of individual or individuating natures of our present world that attempts to draw us back into a joyless future. Our Jessies and Jesuses experienced death because they were dangerous to a culture that wanted to hold on to its power.

Jesus died on the cross for his beliefs, his idea of God, his preaching, his siding with the poor and the outcast. Jesus and all Christ-like persons dared to speak truth to cultural power. This puts us and him in jeopardy.

The words of God never disappear. Words written on paper, words published in books, words spoken, or words hidden inside of the video tapes of our life memories. Words are eternal and we wait to hear them again and again. An old writer said, "The pen is mightier than the sword." Words pry open our minds when we hear them spoken or read them in books. The journey continues in my life.

I transmit my words so that others can build or even change my thoughts or conclusions. My life and work are integrated to heal and joy in my soul. Age is inevitable but it is not a disease nor a disaster. I know that I can do much to live a long, healthy, and vital life. I have lived 80 years. Why not 90? My friends tell me to age gracefully. I want to rumble through this consensual hallucination of my journey to eternity.

Fear of Retirement

Pessimistic old people tell me retirement is worse than death. Retirement scares me more than sickness, poor health, or loss of the ability to share my work with everyone who touches my life. Even though we hold those fears, our lives during retirement can be most fulfilling. Retirement

can be a time for growth, reflection, self-care, and an opportunity to give wisdom of the family. If you have the burden of coming close to outliving any retirement savings to allow you to eat well, travel, work on projects you never had time for with your hours of working full-time.
I want my brief journey to be filled with sounds of laughter. It might even be adorned with a little mischief.

We could well live to be 100 years old. Outliving your money is a realistic fact. We need to exercise to keep our body in shape and our senses alert. Retirement is a daunting risk as we experience declining heath. Health issues increase as we age. We have choices to make so that we are not a burden to our family.

The normal process of getting older has a negative impact on our spiritual, mental, and physical health. Jimmy Carter, my most beloved president, has continued to live with joy and love for the world at nearly 100 years of age. We must understand the things we can control and the things over which we have no control. Use your human energies on what you can control and put your efforts in those realities. Stay committed and consistent and trust and depend on God.

Vocational Gluttony

Perhaps even in ministry, we are guilty of a sin of vocational gluttony. Sometimes it was an economic necessity that I work two or three jobs to make the money required for my family. I would have enjoyed serving any of my pastoral jobs for 50 years. I say I am called to be a communicator. Minister of Joy to the World is what I enjoy calling myself. L. Roger Owens said, "I felt comfortable talking about my vocational confusion." (L. Roger Owens, "Finding a Through Line for My Many Pursuits: Vocational Gluttony," *The Christian Century*, October 6, 2021, pp. 12-13)

Keep listing, keep journaling. Breakdown your goals into small steps for excellent results. If we believe we will live eternally with God in heaven, death will be our door to death, the final part of what we are designed to experience. Keep on being transformed as you will get better and better until the end, or the beginning of eternal joy.

I love what Emily Dickinson wrote:

"This world is not conclusion.
A sequel stands beyond—
Invisible as music—
But positive, as sound."

My life has experienced a satisfaction of discovery and the pleasure of insight during the moments of reading, collecting, discussing life issues with women.

What my masculine soul now knows is reflected in his book. It may be fresh knowledge to many men who struggle. I realize that this knowledge is not completely new, but has been, for me, unarticulated, underground, intuited, and sadly ignored.

As George Eliot wrote, "If we had a keen vision and feeling of all ordinary human life, it would be like hearing the grass grow and the squirrel's heartbeat, and we should die of that roar which lies on the other side of silence." (George Eliot, *Middlemarch*, p. 87)

I have become aware of feminist theory, developmental stages and sequences, and the power of human adaptation and potential. The women in my life painted vivid colorful pictures that made clear my perceptions that had been silenced by some of the institutions where I grew up. I have been thoroughly familiar with the healing of the masculine soul movement. Most of my knowledge has come from other men. Hat is the reason I wrote these differing resources book, because the male experiences have already been articulated. My writing, teaching, and preaching focuses on what men have in common with women. My work examines what else women have to say about the alternate routes that have been missing or sketchy.

Chapter Nine

Living in Joy in the Here and Now

For any woman or man, unhappiness is not being able to love yourself. Happiness is a feeling of contribution, being of value. If your life's calling is interpreted as being recognized by other people, we will have to walk through life with other people's wishes. Any person who is obsessed with recognition does not have a joy of being in community. There is lack of self-acceptance, confidence and trust in others. It is enough to be useful to someone. The present moment is the only reality. Everything that is happening in your life is taking place here and now. Being aware and centered in this current place and time is the only reality. Joy will not surface if we keep on pondering the past or future. Pearl Buck pondered well, "one faces the future with one's past." Lily Langtry nailed it, "Anyone who limits her vision to memories of yesterday is already dead."

We are never too old to learn something new. We can learn something about everything, and we can learn everything about something. I learn something about joy every day. I want to learn at least a little about everything else. That is why I work crossword puzzles with my wife. The answer to clues sometimes eludes us. The world is immense. There is always some new and exciting adventure.

The past is past, and the future is not here yet. The reason that the future will never be here is because it is always something that is unreachable. When tomorrow does arrive, it is not tomorrow, but today. Cherish every moment. Experience each moment for what it is. Slower or unchanging moments are completely present. Immerse yourself in those moments and surprising joy will come.

Women and men become anxious and stressful by thinking about their past or future. We become worn out and out of touch with our true and potential selves. Living with joy in the here and now means to be aware and mindful of what's happening now. Transformation happens as we focus on the present time.

The ability to live in the present time is essential for transformation. Only then can we live in freedom. We cannot change one wee bit of the past. Humans try to relive their past events. We create imaginary scenarios hat are mere dreams. Backtracking is not possible. The only thing we can do with the past is to accept it. This is the same for our future. Despite all our plans, promises, and foresight we cannot program our life journey in advance. We can only receive it moment by moment.

All we have is our present moments.

Here is the only place we are free to act. It is only now that we are in contact with reality. Do we think that the present or future belongs to us? That would create tragic consequences. Holding on for the present will present us with grace. Each moment is sufficient to itself. Read Psalm 145.
Even if our past has been a disaster. Even if our future looks like a dead end. We do not have to be impeded, nor tormented in the future. The joy and freedom and connections between men and women keep us from being oppressed by a burdensome past and a worrisome future. During this time of crises and discontentment, the ideal solution is in one step. It is that step we take today. Whether our annual resolutions produce failure or success, we can begin again te next day.

The effort to rely on one moment is of importance in these changing times bringing injustice and division. We really do not have the capacity to continue suffering for 10, 20, or hundreds of years. We can have the strength to bear today the suffering that belongs to us now. Projecting happening in the future crashes us as we anticipate more suffering. We tend to add regrets about the past and worries for the future. No wonder we live so overwhelmed. We think we have missed many opportunities. Read Matthew 6:25-34. Souls living in anxiety about tomorrow will not be open to the grace of the present moment.

Accept things as they come, one after another. Projecting our fears into the future cuts us off from reality. It saps both our masculine and feminine energies. Joy comes from living, not just waiting to live. People mourn that they don't really have a life. People spend their whole lives waiting to live. Living with joy, every moment is filled.

Envy blocks our unique path to the will of God. Envy and jealousy behave in unpleasant, small, and ugly ways. Envy is clothed in bitterness and resentment, and the drive to bring down those we envy. Envy is a toxic brew that births hatred. Perhaps the root is human inferior complex.

In each encounter with those in our world, we can enjoy the present appointment or calling. We hold a strong sense of proprietary rights to our time. We get upset if we cannot go where we choose. That is the price we pay for keeping our commitments. Life is a succession of moments harmoniously linked.

Each moment is complete in itself. Nothing is left to chance. Our purpose to serve will soon dwindle into nothing unless e have self-control. Obsessed with our yen for power, we can lose sight of those around us and no good can come. Self-control is a needed pre-condition for the flourishing of our souls.

The secret of health for both mind, body, and soul are not to mourn for the past or worry about the future, or anticipate troubles, but to live in the present wisely and passionately. Non-essential possessions free us from the emotions associated with the past. They keep us stuck. Choosing to live in the past or future robs us of joy today. The past has no power over us. Be grateful for the moments of today. Part of te secret is to forgive and move on. Dreaming about the future is only productive when combined with action taken today.

Living in the hear and now requires the courage to be disliked or rejected. Life is a series of moments called now. Every person must live in the here and now. Life exists only in moments. A well-planned life is impossible. There is no one destination for us. Our pasts have nothing to do with here and now. The life journey ahead of us is completely a blank page. There is no certain path for us to follow.

Only in living in the present moment can we exercise our lives. We have no hold on the past. Nobody can ever change the smallest bit of it. We can never backtrack. God is the only eternal presence. Understanding the grace of the present moment is liberating.

God shines in and through us here and now. We might not be aware of it, but She is in our future. Her Spirit waits with patience and love. Human beings are individuals, not things for self-interest. We are social beings that thrive in communion with others. If our community flourishes, we flourish. Our task is to strive for the common good.

Let your soul steady itself. Contemplate your days ahead. View them all as invitations to accept and welcome. You will be helping yourself by living with less stress and patience with the ever-changing world. Worry and rumination are killers of joy. Each moment comes with a life lesson. Each moment is a hidden adventure to be enjoyed.

There is time for building upon our past success. Create more memories for the future you. Our world is changing so rapidly that most of yesterday's solutions are no longer of use to us today. Never get locked into the trap of "that's how we have always done it." Past solutions are not today's solutions. They are certainly not tomorrow's solutions.

We do not have to be religious to be spiritual. Some of the questions below will help in our life transformation: Describe you experience of being a spiritual person.

How do you understand the way that your spirituality has been part of your life?

What has your spirituality led or empowered you to do? What is most important to you about spirituality in your life journey? How is spirituality related to other aspects of your life? In what ways is spirituality related to your sense of your authentic real self?

Honest and sincere integration makes us healthier. It is important to an inner life of balance. Spirituality is related to personal transformation, growth, and empowerment. Spirituality provides an understanding of ourselves related to the sense of meaning and purpose.

Some people will not cooperate. I and my converted colleagues advise you to start, with no regard whether others cooperate or not.

Spirituality enables one to experience joy and happiness. See my book *The Spirituality of Joy* published by Parson's Porch Books. Joy brings contentment or a positive sense to life. Questing for joy has been expressed to me in many words.

"I feel joyful. I feel connected. I feel happy," a person said. "Who am I as a person would be a reflection to spiritual teaching which is honest and sincere." Another smiled and said, "I do want to help others share my experience."

In my research and collection of the descriptions of joy, I found joy internalized and integrated with the core self in relationships, activities, and the life purpose.

We think if we can gain the power to change the world, the world changes. We sometimes feel the world can be changed only by me. The conversion must happen here and now. The shock of someone who has been nearsighted for many years. She puts on glasses for the first time. Indistinct outlines of the world become well defined. Colors are more vivid. We can now see a baseball or tennis ball as we time it so that we can strike it with a bat or tennis racket.

This book and all the books I have published is designed to help my readers know how to help themselves to living in joy. We must give our immediate attention to our surroundings. Accept what opens without tension or judgment. Talk to yourself in the present tense. Never consider that this will happen another day. Practice mindfulness means to practice and express life and to be aware of all our actions.

Part of the women's movement and the transformation of men requires taking more notice of the world. Notice moments surrounding you. Really look at a flower. Gently touch its petals. Do one thing at a time. When I try to write in more than one book project, I miss the mark. Visualize the good things that will be part of your day. If you waste time worrying what might be, and wonder what might have been, you will ignore what is. Each year when I plan my goals for the future next year, I break down the big, huge, and difficult tasks into small and manageable chunks. The size of our goals keeps us focused. I set goals in areas such as preaching, teaching, writing, praying, traveling, counseling and coaching, continuing education, radio and television and internet work.

Look to your graces and gifts and talents to express your joy and share it with as many people as possible. There is not a someday, only now. If your current path holds no joy, take a different path. Your motivation will increase because you will be working in a state of joy instead of feelings of obligation.

Work with your own head-talk. Transformation begins with awareness. Become aware of those automatic thought patterns which lead to automatic behavior patterns. Joy comes not in all relationships, but through loving friending of our colleagues. Joyful people communicate in the deepest sense because they facilitate entry into the souls of others.

The present never ages.

Only you have control over your soul. The life journey with its getting and spending may have been less than successful. Humans have the power to shape souls with feminine and masculine energy. John Barrymore declared, "A person is not too old until regrets take the place of dreams."

The wrinkles in our skin indicate where the smiles of joy have been.

The soul is the total of your essence. The soul comes in your experiences and what you have been doing on your unique journey. When death comes, your soul represents who you were up to the moment you died. The soul leaves a legacy. It is your influence over your relationships. For a physician, it is the impact on the patients. For a writer it's the impact on the readers.

Society is quite sensual which could a difficult place to cultivate courage and self-control. In our cultural context, life is difficult, but not impossible. We have the power to reject what is bad for us and what is good.

Instead of focusing on the time that is running out, now is the time to mark the moment. The present never ages. Every moment is unique to you. Its surprisingness is fully appreciated. Don't postpone your joy. Live in the moments if you can. We choose to become the kind of men and women we are in the end. Freedom springs eternal. Our free will continue to cause growth or mediocre boring lives. Joy is not mediocrity. Joy is not just climbing life's hill halfway but experiencing the summit of it. The common wellspring is the practical good, the spiritual good s revealed in concrete situations. Indestructible unity, not divisive competition, gives us the power to cultivate qualities we have never imagined.

Our cultural environment helps or hinders. If each day is a joyous awakening, we will never grow old.

Be courageous today. Now is the time to contemplate that which is good and noble. Today is the time for love. Today is the only time we have a free and informed decision to love. This decision is not just a sentimental choice. Stand firm in the here and now. Now is the time to dream God's dreams. Now is the time to begin serving God and man unconditionally. Read Mark 10:17-29.

The Joy of Death

Life is here and now. I serve each day to enable people to know that "the joy of the Lord" is our strength. For those who know the essence of all the days we live, dying is not to be feared but a reason for joy. Believing in the love of God in Christ, we know joy is exuberant. Gloria Steinem told us "Dying seems less sad than having lived too little." We cannot choose how we are going to die or the date.

People experience happy deaths even now. The second we are no longer here; we are living in heaven. Ministers bring joy to a funeral. I see joy in death. My concept of joy is not about positive thinking. I have been transformed from always thinking about the future or ignoring the past. The main reason we cannot see joy in death is tat we are not open to it. I still believe that we should be respectful as we perceive a death as tragic. Nothing about death that brings happiness, relief, or gratitude.

Death is a normal and natural part of our life journey. Life on earth has a beginning and an end. Death is part of our lives. It is part of their story and that is important. Memories of the life span stay close to us, even inside of us.

The biggest part of a legacy is the impact their death has on the people they love, as well as those who love he departed. We cannot look for joy in the beginning of our grief. Love is forever. Joy comes in the mourning.

Chapter Ten

LIFE IS NOT A COMPETITION

Trying to become superior is the root to disaster. Sinful humans want to climb life's latter to get higher on the pole. That means we must kick others down.

That is the wrong path to the top. Imagine a stairway and pushing people out of the way. That physical and realistic danger is why Laurel and I invested in an elevator for our new home so we could climb up and down the stairs until we just cannot manage it anymore. The elevator is a symbol of our perseverance.

Competition itself does not bring joy. We do keep score in sports and everything else. In my research on joy, I have asked people to tell me about it. The consensus of the answers showed that helping others, lifting others, and serving others brought joy that is eternal. People are given rewards for their success. The problem is the motive. That is what I am attempting to share with you in this book.

If we live our lives looking for how we can get ahead of others, we are not successful, and joy eludes us. C. S. Lewis expressed it well. He wrote: "The proud make every man their adversary by pitting their intellects, opinions, works, wealth, talents, or any other worldly measuring device against others. Pride gets no pleasure out of having something, only out of having more of it than the next man. It is the comparison that makes you proud, the pleasure of being above the rest. Once the element of competition has gone, pride has gone." (C.S. Lewis, *Mere Christianity*, pp. 109-110)

Some churches think it necessary to count things that we do not need to count. Not everything that can be counted counts. Some are eager to see the numbers of conversions, the money received, how many staff a church reports, and a million little things.

If we tried to count all the inconsequential things we number, it was cause us to be dysfunctional. We count the number of cracks in the sidewalk, the number of stop lights on a trip, the number of SUVs we see, the number of red cars, the number of semi-trucks. Yes, all things are countable, but it is of no help to waste time counting them.

Do not seek ways to compete but savor each unmeasurable joyous experience.

Serene Jones said, "Competition among women is woven into the fabric of a society that has preferred men, so women compete with each other for the attention of men." (Serene Jones, *Call It Grace: Finding Meaning in a Fractured World*, p. 178)

"Extend your vision to include women in order to ore effectively minister to more than half your congregation." (*Ibid.*, p. 163)

The more authentic we are, the less competition we will have. When we are doing what we want to do in life, we can smell the roses along the way. Life is not like a 100-meter dash. It's a marathon. To complete a marathon, we need to join a running group. We might get a coach to improve our stride. Competition is all around us. We do not have to compete. Each life is on its own unique journey. Life is about inspiring others to reach our potential.

Our motive is to find joy. We run outside because it's fun. In Elmwood, Nebraska each year we enjoy see hundreds of people run a fall, more than 1,800 in 2021 in a town of less than 700 population. Women and men who come to run tell us they feel good afterwards.

If one uses energy and time thinking about winning, they also struggle with thoughts of losing. Ina Fey, the actress said, "Do not waste your energy trying to change opinions."

Abraham Maslow could be called minister of transcendence and self-actualization. Maslow's values included playfulness or fun, justice, uniqueness, truth, simplicity, and perfection as excellence.

My daughter Linda shared a project she completed on "Being True to Yourself."
She began with these words: "How do you know if you are on the right path? When we are tapped into our true selves, we will experience synchronicities. The road in life becomes easier; things start to click into place. You might meet someone who will be influential to you at just the right time. When you are living your purpose, you will experience a feeling of expansion like you are opening to something greater. Follow hose feelings. They are your life companions."

We are on the same team. We are not opponents. C.S. Lewis wrote: "Pride gets no pleasure out of having something, only out of having more of it. It is the comparison that makes you proud, the pleasure of being above the rest. Once the element of competition is gone, pride has gone." (C.S. Lewis, *Mere Christianity*, pp. 109-110)

We have no need to compare ourselves with another. Every one of us is unique and different. Appearance, age, knowledge, gender, environment is not the same, but we are equal. Nothing about us is good or bad, superior or inferior. The most productive way of living is to help each one become winners. Being obsessed with competition, victory and defeat, inferior feelings will arise. Everyone becomes your enemy. We begin to believe that people are always looking down on you.

Women and men threat each other with scorn. That world is a terrifying place. People live unhappily with little joy while building success in the eyes of society. Living in competition causes anxiety and we can't celebrate other people's joys.

No matter how much we think we are right, do not criticize the other person on that basis. That is the trap that we fall into. Being convinced that I am right, and you are wrong results in making a power struggle inevitable. Conflicted that I am right includes the assumption that others are wrong. The cultures of politics and religion are attempting to make others submit to them.

Part of the problem is that when either admits to making a mistake that admission means defeat. We choose the wrong path. Only when we turn away the competition can we all win. Joy and balanced energies never come if we attempt to solve problems by ourselves.

Stories of Vocation Could be Gluttonous

"I can certainly see how this scribbling, which sometimes feel indulgent, even gluttonous, belongs right there in the story of my vocation," L. Roger Owens concludes his insightful article. (L. Roger Owens, *The Christian Century*, October 6, 2021, p. 12)

I am alone in my home office writing a manuscript. Writing is an autonomous kind of work. I cannot have someone else do the work in my place. There is the presence of my editor, my close friends, and others without whose assistance this or any other book would come into reality.

People can cooperate even if they do not get along. They have no choice but to cooperate. For example, a man or a woman searches for a job as pastor of a church congregation. They send out resumes, DVDs of their sermons, copies of their books, references, photos, and records of joys and graces and they may even get interviews. Some continue to be rejected. Pride, confidence, and feelings of rejection ooze out. They begin to wonder why they spent a hundred thousand dollars to complete seminary. Why? What is the purpose of serving with our unique gifts if we must go through such things, jumping through the hoops?

Most mature people accept all these obstacles are in themselves not disagreeable. What is disagreeable is being criticized or rebuked by others, getting labeled as having no ability or being incompetent or unsuited for ministry. This hurts the dignity of our irreplaceable selves.

I am sure God laughs at us for our competition atmosphere among pastors. Perhaps instead of losing out on the ministries of hose who have been ejected, send them into places all over the world that are urgently searching for a pastor.

Don't get caught up in waiting on other people to change or the world to change, take the initiative to travel your path. Relationships in which people restrict each other eventually fall apart. Unzipping our souls makes me real, never snobby, but not so humble to have to say, "Pardon my existence."

Intense conversations with clergypersons brought us into positive affirmations. We find it natural to share that life is not a competition. Self-reflection and understanding who we are helps us deal with jealousy. Ours is a ruthless competitive culture. Early in life we are trained to compete. After we get into our perceived purpose, we continue to compete with family members, friends, and professional colleagues.

The negative effect of competition

Today's competition causes jealousy. Our mission is to navigate.

This walled up world can become a perilous place here and now. This is not the fault of other people. It is not the fault of the current atmosphere or environment.
We are responsible for our lifestyle. This involves courage.

Negative competition results in low self-esteem. Transforming these negative comparisons is crucial. We work against the flourishing and fulfillment of other people.

Together we are a source of strength and light. In the past 30 years, I have had women pastors lead male spirituality groups. Women pastors have now asked me to lead in female spirituality groups. We have discovered that this is our most effective way to talk about uncomfortable perspectives. Real transformation happens, and spiritual development is nurtured and experienced. That sacred path helps each person discover the nuances of the journey.

Being in the here and now increases life's meaning as we live fully in the present. Whatever happened in the past does not exist anymore. If you are still talking about what you accomplished yesterday, you haven't understood that not relating to what is real detracts from life's meaningfulness.

Living in the present has a dramatic effect on our spiritual and physical well-being. Living in the present is living in acceptance. Everything is complete as it is. Living in the present means living life with more enthusiasm and joy.

The reality is that people in the world love to compare, compete, and measure success based on accomplishments. Unfortunately, these comparisons rarely bring joy into our lives. The competition leaves us miserable.

Comparisons by their nature are unfair. We should know ourselves more than we know others. Competition is not entirely wrong. We tend to compare the worst we know about ourselves to the best we assume about others. The shallow trinkets we are competing for never bring fulfillment. There are other things we recognize, such as being a loving father or mother, being a faithful spouse, contributing to society, and living a significant and meaningful life. In these noble pursuits in our journey are the desires that matter.

If we refuse to acknowledge these positive things, we will wallow in the dark hole of self-depreciation.

Focus on the Eternal Future in God's Timing.

God has plans for each of us. God's timing is the best. Understand that you are you. You are created you different from everybody else. Where you are now and where you will be wee known by God before you were born.

It is of utmost frustration when nothing changes. Change moves slowly but if does move. Many small changes occur before big changes happen. We make little corrections along the journey. It might appear that nothing is happening, but in God's good time, we discover the change.

It is our human nature to want certainty. Our souls wrestle with the reality of uncertainty. Grace arrives with the mystery that we live out. Trust that mysterious power to create changes needed. God is present in our world. There is no place or time where and when God is not present. God is not counting our sins on a scoreboard. The image of God with that kind of false impression is our projected fear. The joy of salvation is to set us free from that fear. Conversion to Christ brings us to imagine the world as full of kingdom possibilities that we could have missed.

In times of pain and loss, we face our souls. All that we need and all that we are is always present with us. The little suns that reside inside of us await our invitation and invocation.

What we do does make a difference. Our character and our integrity add flames of fire to the agitation in the kingdom of God. Usually what we perceive as a miracle
is the result of many factors. We may focus on any one of the reasons, but it is almost like finding the proverbial nettle in a haystack to know for sure. Some may think that a change came as a result of prayers. Of course, God answers prayers with four answers: Yes. No. Maybe. There is only one God. God is incomparable. Prayer is experienced in silence, in art, and in music. Focus on whatever mustard seedy way we can use for God's answer. God loves us. God works in mysterious ways. Our ways are not God's ways, and our thoughts are not God's thoughts. Focusing on the eternal future means that we ask, seek, and knock for as long as we exist. Things do change. Persistence links life as we keep pounding on heaven's gate, the will of God happens. Diane Sawyer who appears to live in eternal beauty s she grows older and wiser, "What I don't understand is this assumption that aging means isolation. There is just so much to do in this world; so many people who need an ally, so many children who need hugging. I refuse to believe that being elderly and being lonely go hand in hand."

The purpose for which God brought you on this journey is your trip only. Other individuals will be going to some differing places. Joyce Carol Oates said, "We inhabit ourselves without valuing others, unable to see tat here, now, this very moment is sacred; but once it is gone, its value is incontestable." No matter how rapidly we advance in technology, we need to treasure the book. There is nothing in our material world that is more beautiful than a book.

Dear readers, I believe the answers to our problems is for us to walk hand in hand together. Everything I do is for jumpstarting joy in you. I pray my words are an epiphany for you.

AFTERWORD

Jim, when I think about my own spiritual journey, I have been influenced by so many ministers, but you have been one of my most notable blessings. I enjoyed the years that both of us were elected as the moderator of the Christian Church (Disciples of Christ) in Nebraska.

You have touched so many lives and I want to thank you for touching mine. Your joy will continue throughout the remaining years of my life. Whatever our vocation may be, our overall purpose is to introduce people to the "strength of the joy" of Jesus.

I appreciate your support of women in ministry, and the way you created understanding of the feminine value and gave women the same kind of retreat possibilities our Disciples Men have had for so many years.

With your continued prayers, I will try to instill this same joy into others as well. Keep the torch of joy burning with holy passion. Thank you.

~**Kay Koch**, distinguished leader in Nebraska

Jim's book is a call for courage. As minister of Joy to the World, his words have undressed my sense of helplessness. Inequality seems like an unchangeable reality. He has convinced me that nothing is impossible with the joy of the Lord as our strength. The spiritual strength to make it through these challenging times is a precious thing. It is the reason faith is pertinent for faith can move mountains. As a preacher and teacher, Jim has run with grace toward God "to walk and not faint." His new book is a "hot pepper" for future research on equality for demystifying the mistrust both men and women have felt.

~**Pamela Masterson**, Omaha, Nebraska

BIBLIOGRAPHY

Amber, Reuben, *Color Therapy*. New York Aurora Press, 1983.

Belenky, Mary Field, and Blythe McVicker Clinchy, Nancy Goldberger, Jill Tarule. *Women's Ways of Knowing: The Development of Self, Voice, and Mind.* New York: Basic Books, Inc. Publishers, 1988.

Bridges, William. *Making Sense of Life's Changes and Transitions.* New York: Addison-Wesley Publishing Company, 1999.

Brock, Rita N. "An Epidemic of Moral Injury," *Christian Century*, September 8, 2021, pp. 26-30.

Caster, Gary. *Joseph: The Man Who Raised Jesus.* Cincinnati: Servant Press, an imprint of Franciscan Media, 2017.

Christmyer, Sarah. *Becoming Women of the Word: How to Answer God's Call with Purpose and Joy.* Notre Dame, Indiana: Ave Maria Press, 2019.

Cleghorn, John. *Resurrecting Church. Where Justice and Diversity Meet Radical Welcome and Healing Hope.* Minneapolis: Fortress Press, 2021.

Colson, Laura. *Restore the Joy: A Transformation Through Confirmation.* Amazon.com, 2021.

Conway, Jim. *Men in Midlife Crisis.* Fort Worth, Texas: Charrot Victor Publishers, 1998.

Dalby, Gordon. *Healing the Masculine Soul.* Dallas: Word Publishing,
1988.

Dobson, Ted. "Healing the Tear in the Masculine Soul," *Vision*, April 1985, pp. 4-5.

Eliot, George. *Middlemarch*. New York: Penguin Books, 1871, reprinted 1998.

Evans, Rachel Held. Ed. Jeff Chu. *Wholehearted Faith*. New York: Harper One, 2021.

Freed, Betsy Bates and David Freed. "Aversion to Therapy: Why Won't Men Get Help," *Pacific Standard*, June 25, 2012, pp. 12-14.

Frykholm, Amy, "Relational Leadership," *Christianity Today*, Volume 138, Number 9, September 22, 2021, p. 10.

Gallagher, Timothy. *Overcoming Spiritual Discouragement in the Spiritual Life*.
Irondale, Alabama: EWTN Publishing, 2020.

Gates, Melinda French. *The Moment of Lift: How Empowering Women Changes the World*. Seattle: Flatiron Books, 2021.

Gifford, Carolyn DeSwarte, "Nineteenth and Twentieth Protestant Reform Movements in the United States," pp. 294-340. *Women and Religion in America*.
San Francisco: Harper and Row, 1981.

Hammer, Signe. *Passionate Attachments: Fathers and Daughters in America Today*. New York: Rawson Press, 1995.

Hanks, Carl and Fred Rebelsky. "A Father's Verbalization with Infants in the First Three Months of Life," *Child Development*, volume 42, 1971, pp. 63-68.

Harris, Joanne. *Chocolat*. New York: Penguin, 2000.

Hills, Norah. *You Are a Beautiful Rainbow*. Boulder Creek, California: University of the Trees Printers, 1999.

Howes, Lewis. *The Mask of Masculinity*. New York: Rodale Printers, a division of Macmillan, 2018.

Jones, Serene. *Call It Grace: Finding Meaning in a Fractured World*. New York: Viking Division of Random House, 2020.

Keen, Sam. *Fire in the Belly*. New York: Bantam Books, 1996.

Kelly-Gangi, Carol. Editor, *A Woman's Book of Inspiration*. New York: Fall River Press, 2018.

Killinger, John. *Jessie in the Smokies*. Cleveland, Tennessee: Parson's Porch Books, 2008.

Killinger, John. *The Night Jessie Sang at the Opry*. Cleveland, Tennessee: Parson's Porch Books, 2010.

Kishimi, Ichiro and Fumitake Koga. *The Courage to Be Disliked*. New York: Atria Books, 2019.

Lang, Gregory. *Why a Daughter Needs a Dad*. Nashville: Cumberland House Publishing, 2004.

Legato, Marianne. *Why Men Die First: How to Lengthen Your Lifespan*. New York: Saint Martin's Griffon, 2019.

Lewis, C.S. *Mere Christianity*. New York: MacMillan, 1952.

Lorenz, Patricia. *Positive Quotes for Every Day*. Lincolnwood, Illinois: Publications International, 2012.

McCoy, Kathleen. "What Every Man Wishes His Wife Knew," *Redbook* Magazine, October 1985, pp. 142-143.

McKenna, Megan. *Not Counting Women and Children: Neglected Stories from the Bible.* Maryknoll, New York: Orbis Books, 1994.

McReynolds, James. *Joy in the Seasons of Life: Walking Each Other Home to God.* Cleveland, Tennessee, 2021.

McReynolds, James. "Long Distance Parenting," *Christian Single*, January 1990, pp. 36-37.

McReynolds, James. *The Theological Mystery of the Anabaptists.* Elkhart, Indiana: Anabaptist Books, 1970.

Miller, Lisa. "Century Marks: Do-Gooder," *Christian Century*, Volume 138, Number 19, September 22, 2021, p. 8.

O'Neil, James and Jean Egan. "Men's and Women's Gender Role Journeys: A Metaphor for Healing, Transition, and Transformation," *Gender Issues Across the Life Cycle*, ed. Barbara Rubin Wainrib. New York: Springer Publishers, 1992, p. 31.

Osherson, Samuel. *Finding Our Fathers: How a Man's Life Is Shaped by His Relationship with His Father.* New York: Ballantine Books, 1986.

Owens, L. Roger, "Finding a Through Line for My Many Pursuits," *The Christian Century*, October 6, 2021, pp. 11-12.

Payne, Leanne. *Crisis in Masculinity.* Westchester, Illinois: Crossway Books, 1997.

Peck, M. Scott. *The Road Less Traveled.* New York: Touchstone Books, 1990.

Pinkson, Thomas. "Honoring a Daughter's Emergence into Womanhood," *Fathers, Sons, and Daughters*. Los Angeles: Jeremy Tarcher Printers, 1992.

Piper, Mary. *Women Rowing North*. New York: Bloomsbury Publishing Company, 2019.

Reilly, Patricia. *Imagine a Woman in Love with Herself*. New York: MJF Books, 2002.

Robb, Edward. "Is the Church Feminized? An interview with Dr. Donald Joy," *Challenge to Evangelism Today*, Volume 16, number 2, July-August 1989, pp. 1-2.

Roberts, Ronald. "Classical Metaphors for the Transformation of Human Consciousness," *The Journal of Transpersonal Psychology*, Volume 12, number one, 1980, pp. 54-56.

Seidman, Gwendolyn. "Seven Ways You Can Help Your Partner Reach Their Goals," *Psychology Today*, January 5, 2015, pp. 20-24.

Sheehy, Gail. *New Passages: Mapping Your Life Across Time*. Thorndike, Maine: G.K. Hall and Company, 1995.

Smith, David. *The Friendless American Male*. Ventura, California: Regal Books, 1998.

Springer, Sally. *Left Brain, Right Brain*. San Francisco: W.H. Freeman and Company, 1999.

Stockton, Shreve. *Meditations with Cows*. New York: Penguin Random House Teacher Perigee Book, 2021,

Tannen, Deborah. *You Just Don't Understand: Women and Men in Conversation.* New York: Ballantine, 1994.

Thompson, Keith. *The Meaning of Being Male.* Unpublished lecture, 1988.

Toffler, Alvin. *Future Shock.* New York: Bantam Books, 1970.

Vanderbilt, Gloria. *Black Knight, White Knight.* New York: Knopf publishers, 1987.

Verny, Thomas, M.D., *The Secret Life of the Unborn Child.* New York: Summit Books, 2017 edition.

Walker, Alice. *Possessing the Secret of Joy.* New York: Harcourt Brace Jovanovich, 1993.

Williamson, Marianne. *A Woman's Worth.* New York: Random House, 1999.

Wright, Lawrence. "Women and Men: Can We Get Along? Should We Even Try," *Texas Monthly*, February 1996.

Wright, Norman. *Understanding the Man in Your Life.* Waco, Texas: Word Book Publishers, 1987.

Zukav, Gary. *The Seat of the Soul.* New York: Fireside Books and Simon & Schuster, 1990.

About the Author

The minister of joy to the world, Dr. James McReynolds, has done more than any other male to empower women to actualize their potential with love and "the joy of the Lord." His research and insight into the least discussed human emotion has been shared with millions around the globe.

"Truth, Beauty, and Goodness" was the motto of Carson-Newman College. Truth engages the mind. Beauty engages the heart and imagination. Goodness engages us to love deeply. Just four words. This motto is transforming for bring joy into the world.

Dr. McReynolds is a preacher, a prolific writer, healing licensed therapist, and supporter of the masculine and feminine souls. During a School of Practical Christianity in New York, Dr. Norman Vincent Peale anointed him in the oil of joy as the Minister of Joy to the World.

He earned nine academic degrees including five doctor's degrees. He earned his bachelor of arts degree at Carson-Newman University. He earned the bachelor of journalism from the University of Missouri School of Journalism in Columbia.

Midwestern Baptist Theological Seminary awarded him the master of religious education. Luther Rice Theological Seminary in Atlanta presented his the doctor of theology degree. He then earned the master of divinity degree from Vanderbilt University Divinity School. He continued study at Vanderbilt with the doctor of divinity. He was a graduate assistant at Baylor University in the psychology of religion. He earned the doctor of literature from Cardiff Theological College in London. He gained skills in business administration and management with a doctor of philosophy degree from California Coast University. In preparation for doing psychotherapy, Dr. McReynolds received the doctor of psychology recognition in study at the University of Oxford.

Born in Kingsport, Tennessee, he and his parents lived in a one-room apartment. Jim was born on a Tuesday and the following Sunday, he was enrolled in the cradle roll of the First Baptist Church in Kingsport. He was the first person in his family to earn a college degree.

During his lifetime, he has shared his concepts of joy in every nation and territory on the earth. He was ordained at age 12. He has completed nearly 70 years in ordained ministry.

He has enjoyed writing since childhood. He served as public relations specialist for the Sunday School Board of the Southern Baptist Convention. He enjoyed three summers as a summer missionary for the Home Mission Board. With the Foreign Mission Board in Richmond, he was guided as he shared his faith and joy throughout the world.

The author sees joy as Jesus saw the world. His ministry has been beyond the walls and beyond Christian denominations and religions. He has been able to preach and serve as pastor in 12 Christian denominations. He was ordained as a Baptist. Later he was ordained a deacon and elder in the United Methodist Church. In retirement, he has standing with the Christian Church (Disciples of Christ) and other mainline denominations.

Perhaps one way of explaining his prolific life journey would be vocational gluttony.

If your organization would like to invite James McReynolds to speak, his email is joyminister@windstream.net. His website is jamesevansmcreynolds.com. Mailing address is 320 North Fourth Street, Elmwood, Nebraska 68349.

www.ingramcontent.com/pod-product-compliance
Lightning Source LLC
Chambersburg PA
CBHW071452070526
44578CB00001B/316